UNDER THE BLACK FLAG

Simon Bent

UNDER THE BLACK FLAG

THE EARLY LIFE, ADVENTURES AND PYRACIES
OF THE FAMOUS LONG JOHN SILVER
BEFORE HE LOST HIS LEG

OBERON BOOKS
LONDON

First published in 2006 by Oberon Books Ltd
521 Caledonian Road, London N7 9RH
Tel: 020 7607 3637 / Fax: 020 7607 3629
e-mail: info@oberonbooks.com
www.oberonbooks.com

A catalogue record for this book is available from the British
Library.

ISBN: 1 84002 671 5

Printed in Great Britain by Antony Rowe Ltd, Chippenham.

For my brother Paul, Yvette
and Tom

But soft, what light through yonder window breaks?
It is the east, and Juliet is the sun.

Romeo, *Romeo and Juliet*, II: ii: 2–3

This play
in memory of my niece
Sarah Bent, 19 years old
and her boyfriend
Robert Rowbottom, 21 years old
lost on Kho Pi Pi, Thailand
26 December 2004

The play takes place between 1649 and 1660
and is set in England, at sea, North Africa
and the mouth of the Amazon.

CHARACTERS

EXECUTIONER
PRISONER

DIGGER
LEVELLER
FIFTH COLUMNIST
JOHN SILVER
TOM
EBENEZER SILVER
MARY
ANN / ROGER FLINT
CAPTAIN MISSION
HAROLD
OLIVER CROMWELL

KEES DE KEYSER
ONE EYED PEW
BEN GUNN
CALICO JACK
BILLY BONES
BLACK DOG
TEACH
DERBY McGRAW

HAMLET

SULTAN OF MOROCCO
SULA – SULTAN'S DAUGHTER
ISABELLE
ENGLISH AMBASSADOR
FRENCH AMBASSADOR

GENERAL HARRISON

EDWARD
FREDRICK

CITIZENS, ROUNDHEADS, PIRATES, MARINERS,
WORSHIPPERS, OFFICERS, GUARDS

Under the Black Flag was first performed at Shakespeare's Globe, London, on 9 July 2006 with the following company:

TOM, Garry Collins

MARY SILVER / ISABELLE, Jacqueline Defferary

CROMWELL / KING CHARLES / BOSUN, John Dougall

HAROLD / FRENCH AMBASSADOR, Mathew Dunphy

ONE EYED PEW, Trevor Fox

SULA – SULTAN'S DAUGHTER / ANGEL, Akiya Henry

BEN GUNN, Paul Hunter

JOHN SILVER, Cal Macaninch

CALICO JACK / SULTAN OF MOROCCO, Joseph Marcell

BLACK DOG / FREDRICK, Ciaran McIntyre

ANN SILVER, Jane Murphy

EDWARD / BILLY BONES, Paul Rider

HAMLET, Mo Sesay

MISSION / ENGLISH AMBASSADOR, Robin Soans

KEES DE KEYSER, Nicolas Tennant

TEACH / EXECUTIONER, Andrew Vincent

EBENEZER SILVER / GENERAL HARRISON, Howard Ward

Musical Director / Musician, Belinda Sykes

Musicians, Keith Thompson & Jon Banks

Senior Stage Manager, Bryan Paterson

Stage Managers, Vikkie Gibson & Sally Higson

Tiring House Manager, Paul Williams

Deputy Tiring House Manager, David Young

Tiring House Stage Managers, Blair Halliday, Sophie Milne,
   Jason Slack & Tim de Vos

Director, Roxana Silbert

Designer, Laura Hopkins

Composer / Musical Arranger, Orlando Gough

Fight Director, Alison de Burgh

Movement Director, Paul Hunter

Movement Work, Glynn MacDonald

Voice Work, Stewart Pearce

Props Supervisor, Jess Drader

Costume Supervisor, Hilary Lewis

Production Manager, Richard Howey

Wardrobe Manager, Hannah Gunsberger

Wardrobe Deputy, Elaine Taylor

Wardrobe Support Deputy, Bob Capocci

Wardrobe Assistants, Eleanor Dolan & Katherine Buck

Wigs, Hair and Make-up Managers, Pam Humpage & Louise Ricci

ACT ONE

ONE

Scaffold. A masked EXECUTIONER with an axe. SOLDIERS. Drums.

Enter a PRISONER. Blindfold and hands tied. Led onto the scaffold. Hands untied. Blindfold removed. Silence.

PRISONER: Bear witness. I forgive the world.

EXECUTIONER takes a practice swing and brings axe down into chopping block.

I forgive the world, and all those that are the causes of my death. Who they are, God knows, I do not desire to know. God forgive them. Cromwell, 'You are the great robber, I am but a petty thief.' I die a Christian. I go from a corruptible to an incorruptible crown, where no disturbance can be, no disturbance in the world.

Takes off cloak and doublet, rips open his shirt at the neck.

I am the martyr of the people.

Led to block and neck put on it.

Silence. EXECUTIONER bends toward him.

Stay for the sign.

EXECUTIONER: Yes, I will, an' it please Your Majesty.

Clears PRISONER's neck of hair. Stands ready. Drums.

Silence.

PRISONER thrusts his hands forward.

His head chopped off.

TWO

Crowd of CITIZENS. Enter JOHN SILVER and TOM.
Song: FREEDOM

CITIZENS: The King is dead
    O joyful day
    More beer

> (*Chorus.*) **Freedom**
> **Freedom**
> **Freedom**
> **More beer**
>
> **Republicans**
> **The Commonwealth**
> **More beer**
>
> (*Chorus.*)
>
> **Cromwell tyrant**
> **Parliament traitors**
> **More beer**
>
> (*Chorus.*)

Crowd roars approval.

TOM: You lost him…

SILVER: I woke up and he was gone.

TOM: Where were you…

SILVER: In a ditch.

TOM: You lost your father.

SILVER: That's right, so now I'm in charge. (*Shouts.*) Babylon falls, Glory rises.

LEVELLER: Be not afraid.

DIGGER: What's at stake is the ownership of England.

ALL: Cromwell – Parliament – Tyrants – Traitors – Kings.

Enter EBENEZER SILVER from the back of the pit.

EBENEZER: John Silver.

TOM: Now you're for it.

EBENEZER: John Silver.

SILVER: Father.

EBENEZER: No son of mine.

SILVER: At last, I've found you.

EBENEZER: Take my place. Never. Left me for dead. Give me your hand.

They help him up.

I'd rather a dog.

EBENEZER strikes SILVER to the ground.

CITIZENS: They enclose our land – they take our homes – we are being robbed.

DIGGER: In Cromwell I fear we have chosen an oppressor to redeem us from oppression.

FIFTH COLUMNIST: The King is dead, long live the Republic.

LEVELLER: God levels all.

CITIZENS: Aye – aye – God is no respecter of persons – we are all equal.

SILVER: I don't like it.

EBENEZER: Aye, they're an ugly bunch. Radicals.

SILVER: Not them, working for you.

EBENEZER: Go it alone then.

SILVER: I will. All you have to do is shout and take people's money.

EBENEZER: Crumb of a man.

DIGGER: And who are the oppressors but the gentry, the nobility, and we the oppressed, the yeoman, the farmer, the tradesman, the labourer. Your slavery is their liberty. Your poverty their prosperity.

TOM: Who are we shouting for again.

EBENEZER: Wait for it. I've worked hard on this character – he's after my old school-master.

Turns away. Then turns round with a hat on his head.

There. The right holy, the right godly, right saintly, right reverend Ebenezer Coppse who has been sent in search of saints.

SILVER: I see no difference.

TOM: And where have you been sent from.

EBENEZER: The Kingdom of Heaven.

CITIZENS: Tell us the news – what news – they tell us nothing.

CITIZEN 1: They've closed the theatres.

CITIZEN 2: And made adultery illegal.

SILVER: (*Shouts back.*) It already is.

EBENEZER: (*As Coppse.*) Now let the axe fall upon Cromwell's neck. Now we set England free from the yoke of tyranny.

SILVER / TOM: Yoke of tyranny.

Frenzied crowd roars approval.

CITIZEN 2: Sleep with my wife and they'll hang you.

SILVER: Sleep with my wife and you can have her.

EBENEZER: I already have and I don't want her.

Takes off hat.

Enough of that. The world's gone mad.

SILVER: This is what happens when you sever the head off the body politic; the country charges about wild like a headless chicken in the barnyard until it's grown back another one.

EBENEZER: You've learnt your speeches.

SILVER: No.

TOM: Yes.

SILVER: Nearly.

EBENEZER: Recite me some.

SILVER: (*Recites.*) 'I am a saint and I am sent to declare that sin and transgression is ended – '

EBENEZER: With feeling.

SILVER: (*Shouts.*) 'I am a saint – '

EBENEZER: Not so loud.

SILVER: (*Softer.*) 'I am a saint – '

TOM / SILVER: (*Together.*) 'And I am sent to declare that sin and transgression is ended – I am His saint – sent to declare... declare the Word, His Word – '

EBENEZER: Alright, alright. When I say 'Who dare', you say –

SILVER: I dare.

TOM: I dare.

EBENEZER: With feeling lads, with feeling, you're agreeing to becoming saints, embracing the Kingdom of Heaven.

TOM: When do we get paid.

EBENEZER: After. One crown.

TOM: You said half a crown.

SILVER: It's gone up.

EBENEZER: No, one crown as agreed.

SILVER: What if the Roundheads come.

EBENEZER: The Fighting Cocks at supper.

TOM: And what is it you're supposed to be preaching for again.

EBENEZER: Drinking, gambling, dancing, lying with one another, kissing – Fornication.

SILVER: I'll convert to that.

EBENEZER: Sin, the truest and most direct path to God.

TOM: What if we get caught.

EBENEZER: Just play your part to the end, no matter what. They'll cajole you, they'll threaten you, they've even put me in front of a firing squad before now – but you play the holy fool and they always let you go. They never shoot anyone. Got it.

SILVER: Got it.

TOM: Got it.

EBENEZER: Don't forget to take your clothes off.

TOM: And how do we take their money?

EBENEZER: That's what the hat's for.

TOM: Clever.

SILVER: Pretty obvious if you ask me.

EBENEZER stands above crowd.

I'm not taking my clothes off.

TOM: You said half a crown.

DIGGER: I fear all men that would be King.

EBENEZER: Cause a disturbance.

SILVER: You mug of custard.

TOM: Jug of monkey cum.

SILVER: Lick my arse.

EBENEZER puts on hat.

EBENEZER: He has sent me in search of saints. Damnation is coming.

SILVER: (*Shouts.*) More beer.

CITIZENS: Let him speak, let them speak.

TOM: Get me a drink.

SILVER: Drink my cum.

TOM: You said half a crown.

SILVER: Lick my paps.

TOM: Jug of monkey cum king.

SILVER knocks TOM to ground. They fight.

EBENEZER: Judgement Day has come. We fight among ourselves.

Enter MARY with bucket of water.

MARY: John Silver.

EBENEZER: The end is truly coming.

MARY: John Silver.

EBENEZER: Embrace it with open arms.

MARY: Mister.

EBENEZER: The power and the glory, forever and ever, Amen.

CITIZENS: Amen.

EBENEZER: Let us pray.

All pray but for SILVER, TOM and MARY.

MARY: Mister.

Throws bucket of water on TOM and SILVER.

I must be damned.

SILVER: No, it is I that am damned.

MARY: Damned to have married you.

SILVER: Mary.

MARY: Don't you Mary me, John Silver. Going about the countryside drinking, fighting, taking your clothes off –

TOM: We're celebrating.

MARY: Fornicators. He's got a wife and child to feed. Damn you.

SILVER: I'm damned already.

TOM: Aye, that's right, he is.

SILVER: Aye.

TOM: You are.

SILVER: I am.

TOM: He is.

SILVER: Aye.

TOM: Aye.

SILVER: It was marrying her that made me realise I was damned.

TOM: Give it to her.

SILVER: Aye.

TOM: Aye.

MARY: You are an hypocrite, a revolter, a back-slider.

TOM: Go on, slap her.

MARY: I'll slap you Tom Piper, see if I don't – from here to kingdom come.

TOM: I'll land you one myself if you don't watch it.

MARY: Come on then.

SILVER: Go on.

MARY: You're drunk.

SILVER: I've had a drink, we've had a drink, a man's entitled to his drink.

TOM: It's fortunate for you that he is my friend.

MARY: Such good fortune.

TOM: Witch.

MARY: (*At TOM.*) Bargh!

She chases him.

TOM: Keep her in line, you've got work to do.

Exit TOM.

SILVER: No, Tom, Tom.

MARY: A curse on the day I married you.

SILVER: Don't go, Tom.

MARY: You should have married Tom.

SILVER: Aye, nature's cruel.

MARY: Don't push me, mister.

SILVER: Go on, leave.

MARY: No one to fetch and carry for you.

SILVER: I don't need you.

MARY: I don't need you.

SILVER: Go on, leave.

MARY: I will.

SILVER: Go on.

MARY: I am.

SILVER: Go.

MARY: I'm going.

SILVER: Take my daughter, take little Ann with you.

MARY: I will.

SILVER: And my dog. Take everything, leave me with nothing, see if I care.

MARY: There's nothing to take.

SILVER: All would be well with me.

MARY: As well as it was with Judas who repented and hanged himself.

SILVER: I'd land on my feet.

MARY: Or on your back in a ditch.

SILVER: You won't let me in the house.

MARY: You're always drunk.

SILVER: So now I'm not allowed to enjoy myself.

MARY: You've got a daughter to feed.

SILVER: I love my daughter, don't tell me I don't love my daughter, I love her more than anything else in the world, I'll do anything for my daughter, I'd die for her, I'll give up my life for her.

MARY: Just come home.

SILVER: Love, my love.

Goes to kiss MARY.

MARY: No, don't.

SILVER: I missed you.

MARY: That's why you stopped out all week.

SILVER: I know. I know.

MARY: Well, at least you're not up to no good with that lying cheating father of yours. He's nowhere to be found either.

SILVER: Forgive me.

MARY: Stop looking at me like that.

SILVER: What, what.

MARY: I'm not smiling. This isn't funny.

SILVER: I know.

MARY: It's not funny.

SILVER: Forgive me.

MARY: Stop drinking.

SILVER: I will.

He kisses her.

Enter ANN.

ANN: They've chopped off the King's head.

SILVER: Ann, Annie, my little Ann – come and give me a kiss.

ANN: I don't kiss strangers.

MARY: See, even your daughter's forgot who you are.

SILVER: Come on little Annie, give me a kiss. I've got a secret.

ANN: I don't care.

SILVER: Come here and I'll whisper it to you.

ANN: No. You'll spit in my ear.

SILVER: No, I won't.

ANN: You always say that.

SILVER: I've got a surprise for you.

Fishes in pocket. Holds out fist, clenched. ANN drawn to it. SILVER withdraws fist.

First my secret.

ANN: You'll spit in my ear, he'll spit in my ear.

MARY: I'll spit in his ear if he does.

SILVER: Come on Ann.

ANN: You promise not to spit.

SILVER: I won't spit.

She goes to him.

That's a good girl.

He spits in her ear.

ANN: He spit in my ear. You spat in my ear. You promised.

SILVER: I never.

ANN: He promised.

SILVER: I never. I never promised anything.

MARY: No you never do.

SILVER: Here, look what I got you.

ANN: I don't want it.

SILVER: A ring.

ANN: Liar, liar –

SILVER: Come on, love...

ANN: I don't like it – liar, liar, liar, you'll go to hell for that, you're going to Hell, you'll burn in Hell.

Exit ANN.

SILVER: Ann, Ann, Annie, little Ann. You've forgot your ring.

MARY: Leave her.

SILVER: What, what did I do, I haven't done anything.

MARY: No you don't, you've never done a day's work in your life.

SILVER: I work.

MARY: No, you don't.

SILVER: I do, I work. I'm working now.

MARY: This isn't work, this is petty thievery – converting to any cause that will pay you enough to keep you in beer money.

SILVER: I work.

MARY: When. You say it's parliament that don't work, you say it's the Church that don't work, but it's you that don't work. Any excuse. Like father, like son.

EBENEZER rises from prayer.

EBENEZER: Damnation is coming.

SILVER: (*To MARY.*) What do you want me to do.

MARY: Come home now.

Enter TOM.

SILVER: I can't.

EBENEZER: The end is near. Embrace it with open arms.

MARY: Put food on the table.

She goes to exit.

SILVER: Mary, no Mary –

MARY: Don't.

EBENEZER: He has sent me in search of saints.

MARY: I know that voice.

SILVER: Mary.

EBENEZER: Who here will dare face persecution.

MARY: It is, it's him.

SILVER: Mary.

EBENEZER: Let him who dare say 'I do' go naked before the Lord.

CITIZEN 1: Get off.

CITIZEN 2: Go home.

CITIZEN 3: Enough.

EBENEZER: Who dare.

TOM: (*Shouts.*) I dare.

CITIZEN 2: Descend.

CITIZEN 1: Stand down

CITIZEN 3: Go.

EBENEZER: Who else dare say 'I dare'.

MARY: You choose, him or me.

EBENEZER: Who else among you.

SILVER: (*Shouts.*) Me, I dare.

MARY: Your choice.

SILVER: No, Mary, no – he truly believes that he's a saint.

EBENEZER: Now let those who dare say 'I dare' say 'I do'.

TOM: I do.

MARY: Come home.

SILVER: I can't.

EBENEZER: Who dare say 'I do'.

SILVER: Me, I do.

The crowd cheer and clap with approval. Exit MARY.

Mary.

EBENEZER: Men shall say you are not only a lunatic but quite beside yourself –

CITIZEN 4: Lunatics.

Laughter.

CITIZEN 3: More beer.

EBENEZER: Amen, Hallelujah, Hallelujah, Amen.

TOM: This is your speech, now it's you.

SILVER: I am in the belly of Hell, I am among all the devils in Hell – and under all this terror, there I see, I see, a spark of transcendence, transplendent, unspeakable glory triumphing, exalting, confounding, all the blackness of darkness – and I am in tears, in tears, out of this body, wiped out, swept up – breath and life, light, lights, various streams of light, exceeding brightness – swallowed up into unity; within and without, unity, universality, universality, unity, Eternal Majesty. I return to my mother's womb, naked, out of which I had once come naked blinking in the light. And a voice, a most strong, glorious voice speaks to me – the strong hand of eternal, invisible almightiness is stretched out upon me, within me – and voices, more voices – 'Blood, blood', 'Where? Where?', 'Upon the hypocritical holy heart', 'Vengeance, vengeance, vengeance', 'Plagues, plagues upon the inhabitants of the earth' –

Falls to ground.

'Fire, fire, fire', 'Sword, sword, sword – upon all that bow not down to Eternal Majesty, universal love.'

Silence.

EBENEZER: That's right, lad – now take your clothes off.

CITIZEN 1: Witchcraft.

CITIZEN 2: Devil.

CITIZEN 3: Possessed.

EBENEZER: Oh, dear hearts, open, for I, the King of Glory am coming in to anoint thee and am loath to be arrested for burglary – you will never fall from grace because you are His saint and a true saint is incapable of sin. There is no sin. Take off your clothes and go naked as saints among the crowd, before the Lord. Behold, behold –

CITIZEN: He's taking his clothes off.

Drumming offstage.

CITIZENS: The Roundheads are coming – Cromwell's press gang – the new model army.

Whistling and caterwauling.

Enter CAPTAIN MISSION, HAROLD and ROUNDHEAD SOLDIERS.

MISSION: Get home. Disperse. Load muskets.

SOLDIERS load muskets.

Back to your homes, back to your labours. Present arms.

SILVER: Run lads, The Fighting Cocks at supper.

All three exit.

SOLDIERS aim muskets at crowd.

Away.

Draws sword and raises it above head.

Take aim.

SOLDIERS cock their barrels.

Fire.

ROUNDHEADS shoot a volley of musket shots above the heads of the crowd.

MISSION: After them, Harold.

HAROLD: Yes, father.

MISSION: After them and round up their leaders for impressment and spiriting away to the colonies.

HAROLD: Is that an order father.

MISSION: Just get on with it boy.

HAROLD: Yes father.

Drums. Enter CROMWELL.

Song: THE MORAL ARMY

ROUNDHEADS: **We are the major model**
    Of a modern moral army
    The major moral model
    Of a very modern army

MISSION: General, my Lord Cromwell, sir.

CROMWELL: The crowd is dispersed.

MISSION: Yes, General. As you instructed.

CROMWELL: All that we do, we do for God, Captain Mission.

MISSION: My Lord Cromwell.

Enter HAROLD and ROUNDHEADS with TOM and EBENEZER naked.

TOM: I aren't a radical.

CROMWELL: Hold your tongue. This conflux of dissidence is a many headed hydra and may be a beginning from which things of greater and more dangerous consequence to the Commonwealth will grow.

TOM: I'm innocent.

CROMWELL: We are all guilty.

MISSION: On your knees and beg forgiveness.

EBENEZER: I kneel before no man.

CROMWELL: Cover your nakedness.

EBENEZER: We stand equal before the Lord.

MISSION strikes EBENEZER with musket butt, EBENEZER falls to knees.

TOM: He's got nothing to do with me…

TOM drops to knees.

EBENEZER: Kiss us, warm us, feed us, cloth us, money us, relieve us, take us into your houses, don't serve us as dogs. We are your flesh, your brethren.

CROMWELL: You are no brethren of mine. Blasphemer, drunk, fornicator.

EBENEZER: Sin, the straightest, most true path to God.

MISSION strikes EBENEZER.

TOM: I was just acting a part.

Enter SILVER.

SILVER: There you are. I've been looking all over. Who's in charge.

CROMWELL: I am. Who are you.

SILVER: John Silver, sir. Charged with the care of this debauch old man and deluded fool.

CROMWELL: What do you want.

SILVER: To relieve you of their burden captain.

CROMWELL: Take them to the ship.

TOM: Press ganged.

SILVER: Oh, to serve my country again, to take up a musket and carry a pike in defence of the Commonwealth – Marston Moor, Naseby and last but not least Preston. Would that I could...but I am forbid from risking my life again, which I would gladly give ten times over, forbid so that I should look after my wife, blinded by Cavaliers while they raped her and plundered my farm, forbid so that I should look after my daughter who suffers from the 'falling sickness', who bit her own tongue clean off while writhing on the ground and foaming at the mouth with her mother groping in the dark to save her when I was at market one day, forbid by Cromwell himself after the Battle of Langport, during which my leg accidentally saved his life as he lay winded on the ground and it got in the way of a Royalist musket shot intended for his heart. I pleaded with him, I swore, I wept, I begged him not to forbid me from taking up arms again

– but he said I could best serve my country by going home and looking after my despoiled wife and afflicted daughter. He made me vow and sent me off back home limping to my family. I didn't want to say any of this sir, but felt needs you must know, for fear of offending Oliver Cromwell himself and bringing misery unwittingly on yourself.

MISSION: I'm going to enjoy breaking you.

CROMWELL: Reward this man for his bravery, captain.

SILVER: So, you aren't the captain, sir.

CROMWELL: No, I am not.

SILVER: Who are you then.

CROMWELL: Oliver Cromwell.

MISSION strikes SILVER to ground with musket butt.

EBENEZER: Repent, repent, repent, bow down, bow or howl, resign or be damned.

CROMWELL: God is my master, and the Bible my word.

EBENEZER: The Bible is not the word of God.

CROMWELL: Shoot him. Blasphemer. And when you look on the face of God, tell Him I sent you.

Drums. Exit CROMWELL.

MISSION: Take these two to the ship.

SILVER: I can't – I've a wife and child.

MISSION: And shoot the old man.

EBENEZER: I am a saint. And these my apostles.

TOM: No, no – we were just acting a part – we're very good at acting me and John.

EBENEZER: Lo and I say unto you act as saints, fear not the part in which you have been cast, uphold your role as 'saint' and you'll come to no harm.

SILVER: Forgive me Lord for I have sinned. I am a saint.

EBENEZER: Truly you are a saint.

SILVER: And I am sent by the Lord.

TOM taken off.

TOM: Farewell England.

MISSION: Ready old man.

EBENEZER: Wait.

MISSION: Present arms.

EBENEZER: Heaven and Hell, the Resurrection and the Final Judgement, are all part of a man's life.

MISSION: Finished…

EBENEZER: Go forth and spread the word.

SILVER: I am a saint.

EBENEZER: You are a saint.

SILVER: Shoot me.

EBENEZER: No shoot me.

SILVER: Shoot me.

EBENEZER: No, shoot me.

SILVER: No, shoot me.

MISSION raises pistol and shoots EBENEZER himself.

Father. You shot my father.

MISSION: I'm going to enjoy breaking you, 'saint'. The Lion's Whelp.

SOLDIER: Aye, captain.

MISSION: Come, away now Harold, we go to prayer, then sail for Jamaica.

HAROLD: Yes, father.

Exit MISSION and HAROLD. Exit SILVER and SOLDIER.

SILVER: Father.

SOLDIER: Scurvy swab.

SILVER: Father. He shot my father.

Exit SILVER. SOLDIERS drag EBENEZER off.

THREE

At sea. The deck of The Lion's Whelp.

BOSUN, MISSION, TEACH. TEACH with a lash. HAROLD upstage with spyglass, looking out to sea.

Song: THE SEA

SAILORS: **The sea, the sea, the sea**
And more sea
In every direction the sea

HAROLD: The sea, the sea, the sea and more sea. I never
thought it possible to see so much sea. In every direction –

SAILORS: **The sea, the sea, the sea**
And more sea
In every direction the sea

HAROLD: This wooden hull The Lion's Whelp our vessel,
her deck below a stage for all the world to see, cast upon
the waters of this orb we call the Globe, in transport
and suspension across the Seven Seas beyond the Seven
Wonders to stories not yet told – in search of distant shores
– some remembered, others half forgot, some lying in wait
we come at through a mist, and suddenly crashed upon their
rocks.

SAILORS: **The sea, the sea, the sea**
And more sea
In every direction the sea

HAROLD: And through this eyeglass we glimpse as at ourselves,
strangers in a strange and yet familiar land, mapping out the
geography and limits of our lives.

MISSION: Next.

BOSUN: Silver, John Silver, sir and his friend Tom, theft of ship's
biscuits. Silver.

SILVER dragged on and tied to whipping post.

HAROLD: Blown off course early on – these last few days a
stagnant calm – mutiny is in the air – the men grow restless
–the more at sea the more the floggings. A ship. An English

29

merchant-ship, billowing smoke, in distress. Her decks are empty. A one-eyed sailor tied to the wheel. She's coming this way.

TEACH flogs SILVER.

TEACH: Forty eight. This is hard work.

MISSION: But necessary.

HAROLD: Can I come down now father.

MISSION: Just you keep an eye on that ship, Lieutenant.

HAROLD: I do have a name father.

MISSION: Forty-nine.

TEACH: Forty-nine.

HAROLD: I'm coming down.

MISSION: Keep watch or I'll have you flogged.

HAROLD: I'm your son.

TEACH: Hanging's easier than this.

MISSION: Flogging's good for morale.

TEACH: Fifty.

HAROLD: She's billowing smoke, father.

MISSION: Prepare the ship's doctor for a sudden influx of the sick and injured, Bosun.

BOSUN: Aye, aye captain.

Exit BOSUN.

TEACH: That's him done.

MISSION: What say you now, saint.

SILVER: We were hungry.

MISSION: Are you complaining.

SILVER: No, sir, we never complain. I am bitter cold, and hungry.

MISSION: That sounds like complaining to me.

SILVER: We need feeding. So as we eat we work. It's not our business to starve. And if you think it is, then hanging can be little worse.

MISSION: Then I'll hang you, keel haul you, balls first.

TEACH: I don't think my back is up to a keel hauling, captain.

HAROLD: Ship, ho.

MISSION: (*Looks up.*) Ship ahoy, lieutenant.

SILVER: Murderer.

MISSION: What was that, saint.

SILVER: You heard.

MISSION: Another fifty lashes Mister Teach.

HAROLD: Coming up along side the English merchant, father.

TEACH: It's getting dark, maybe we should hold off the rest of the floggings till tomorrow – or switch to hanging.

Creaking of ship's deck and ropes.

HAROLD: She's coming up alongside us.

SILVER: 'Tis the hour for spirits. When all the dead we have ever done harm to rise up from the grave and come back to haunt us and deprive us of sleep. How much sleep do you get, captain.

MISSION: If there's any justice in the world you shall get your throat cut or be famished, whatever way I'm going to make sure you never get back again over the great pond.

SILVER: We are all tadpoles.

MISSION: You think this is funny, saint.

SILVER: No, sir, captain, sir. We are all tadpoles in the great pond of life. And given half the chance I'll kill you.

MISSION: One hundred lashes…

TEACH: My back.

HAROLD: (*Looking through spyglass.*) Her decks are empty. She's like a ghost ship. What's this – she's raising her gun flaps…

Sudden blast of cannon shot broadside. Blunderbuss and pistol shot. Ship's bell.

SAILORS: (*Off.*) What ho! – Thieves thieves – The Turk.

Enter SAILORS, cutlasses drawn.

SAILOR 1: The Turk.

SAILOR 2: What ho! What ho foul thief.

MISSION: Pagan moors, infidel Turks, renegade freebooters, the scourge of God.

Draws sword.

I'll hang you after.

BOSUN: Pirates – we're under attack – pirates – it's a trap – save yourselves first.

MISSION: Shoot any man that surrenders. Draw your sword Harold and fight.

HAROLD: Yes, father.

MISSION: And if we are taken, let no one know that you are my son.

HAROLD: Yes father.

KEES, GUNN and PEW (pirates) swing in and slide down on ropes.

PIRATES: (*Sing.*) **Liquor, Gold**
Booty, Slaves
Women

KEES: Take no prisoners.

MISSION: Black Devils.

PEW, GUNN and KEES fight MISSION, TEACH and HAROLD.

KEES disarms MISSION, levels sword at his throat.

KEES: Raise the black flag. Cut that man down.

PEW cuts SILVER down. TOM pushed on deck.

The Whelp is ours. Where's your captain.

MISSION: I am.

PEW: Burn him.

KEES: Aye. And the souls and bodies of the blood suckers who own him, to fry in the fire of hell. Damn them for a pack of rascals, and damn you who serve them, you hen-hearted numbskull. They vilify us, when there is only this difference – they rob the poor under cover of law, while we plunder the rich under protection of our own courage. Had you not better make one of us then, than sneak after these villains for employment?

MISSION: My conscience will not allow me to break the laws of God.

KEES: You are a devilish conscience rascal. I am a free prince, free to wage war on the whole world, free as he who has one hundred sail of ship or one thousand armies of men in the field. And this my conscience tells me.

MISSION: Honour thy father honour thy mother, a maxim that extends to my country now.

SILVER: Who is a right father, a right mother to a bastard like you.

MISSION: Cromwell and the Commonwealth.

KEES: I would rather Satan the Sultan of all Hell.

MISSION: Christians are made Turks and Turks are sons of devils.

KEES: Which one of you will turn Renegado. Speak. No beggars or the lash among us – and the world to come is a boundless kingdom, that lieth all open; Heaven on Earth, now.

SILVER: Aye, count me in.

GUNN: Well chose shipmate, have a bit of cheese.

PEW: Just keep your cheese to yourself.

GUNN: Alright, I will.

PEW: Good.

CALICO: Pipe down, the pair of you.

KEES: Who else is for us.

GUNN: Don't you ever come sniffing about me for a bit of cheese Pew, never again.

PEW: I won't.

GUNN: Because you won't get any.

PEW: I don't want any.

GUNN: Never again.

PEW: Good, I'd rather slit my own throat.

GUNN draws dagger.

GUNN: I'll slit it for you if you like.

CALICO: Just pipe down.

GUNN: Calico Jack.

CALICO: Yes, Ben Gunn.

PEW: Aye, Calico Jack.

CALICO: Yes, Mister Pew.

GUNN / PEW: (*Together.*) Fuck off.

PIRATES laugh.

KEES: I say again, who's for us and who's against us.

SILVER: Come on, Tom.

TOM: No, no, I can't –

SILVER: Heaven on earth, now – it's mighty tempting, Tom.

TOM: Yes it is, and I appreciate the offer, really I do, but I'll
    wait.

BLACK DOG: For what.

TOM: Until I'm dead.

BLACK DOG: Are you asking. Is he asking.

SILVER: No, no, he's not. Are you sure Tom, sure you don't
    want to go a-pirating about the seven seas with me and Mr
    One Eyed Pew.

GUNN: Mister Pew.

TOM: No, I can't.

KEES: Then it's slavery you choose, clap him in irons.

TOM: No, I have to go home.

KEES: Slave.

TOM shackled.

PEW: He has to go home.

PIRATES laugh.

BONES: I haven't been home for five years.

BLACK DOG: I ain't never going home again in my life.

GUNN: You burned your home to the ground Billy Bones.

BONES: I had no choice.

SILVER: Why's that then, sir, Mister Bones.

BONES: Tell him.

BLACK DOG: I will. Because one black night he took a carving knife to his wife and filleted her on the kitchen table.

BONES: She had it coming.

PEW: He carved up his entire family and cooked them into a stew.

BLACK DOG: Then burned down his home.

BONES: Least I had one to burn down.

PEW: Unlucky in love, lucky in life.

BONES: Aye.

PEW: I've never had much luck in either direction.

GUNN: It broke my mother's heart when first I left, weeping and wailing and tearing at her breasts on the quayside.

PEW: Tears of joy.

BLACK DOG: Newgate gaol is my mother and the gallows my father.

BONES: She had it coming. (*Spits.*) Cut me a quid of tobacco, lad.

SILVER: Aye. Sir. Look, he'll be a pirate, alright. Won't you, lad.

TOM: Yes, yes I will.

KEES: Too late lad, you had your chance; you're worth more to us as a slave. Take him away.

TOM: Jug of monkey cum king.

They go to take TOM away.

SILVER: Lay hands on him and you will suffer, captain.

KEES: I will suffer.

SILVER: Yes, you will suffer.

KEES: You hear that lads, I'm going to suffer.

BLACK DOG: The captain's going to suffer, lads.

PIRATES laugh.

KEES: Make me suffer; pain and suffering is my currency.

SILVER: I am a saint.

MISSION: He's no saint.

SILVER: A true saint.

MISSION: A blasphemous saint, hang him.

SILVER: Behold – behold – a vengeful God, He will destroy you, smote you with fire, plague you with boils, eternal suffering, or set him free, and me.

KEES: Where's your halo.

SILVER: Everlasting pain.

KEES: I know what misery is lad, I inflict it.

PIRATES: Turn water into wine – smote him with fire – deliver us from evil – kill the swine.

KEES: Fight me. Here, I give you my sword.

SILVER: God is my master.

KEES: Fight me. Or, convert me.

MISSION: Hang him. He's no saint. Hang the blasphemer.

KEES strikes MISSION.

KEES: You, saint, what do I do with this wretch.

MISSION: Blasphemous seducer and black-magician sent by God to punish all back-sliding Christians.

KEES strikes MISSION to the deck.

PEW: Burn him –

GUNN: Make him walk the plank.

MISSION: Do your worst.

KEES: Aye, captain, you can be sure of that.

KEES kicks MISSION.

(*To SILVER.*) You saint. You choose. He had you flogged.

SILVER: He murdered my father, shot him in cold blood.

KEES offers SILVER pistol.

KEES: Revenge.

SILVER takes pistol.

Do him.

MISSION: Do it.

KEES: Blow off his face.

HAROLD: Do and you're damned, Silver.

MISSION: Keep out of this, lieutenant.

SILVER: Don't and I'm damned.

KEES: Show no mercy. He deserves it. Between the eyes.
Murderer.

SILVER aims pistol.

MISSION: That's right. Look me in the eyes.

Silence.

Go on.

HAROLD: No.

KEES: Do it.

MISSION: No. You won't. He couldn't. You can't. And when I get
back to England I'll find your wife and child and hang them.

SILVER lowers pistol.

Shoot me.

SILVER: You killed my father, and now you will kill my wife and
daughter.

MISSION: It will be my pleasure.

SILVER cocks pistol.

HAROLD: Father.

SILVER: Your son.

MISSION: He's not my son.

SILVER: Then it won't matter.

SILVER aims pistol at HAROLD.

MISSION: No.

SILVER shoots HAROLD.

HAROLD: Father, I am shot.

HAROLD drops dead. SILVER vomits. PIRATES laugh.

GUNN: Have a bit of cheese lad; fortify your choler.

PEW: He doesn't want cheese.

KEES: How about the captain, lad.

MISSION: Better you had kill me as well Silver, I live and I will come after you.

SILVER: No. Now suffer.

GUNN: The wisdom of Solomon.

PEW: And he's clever.

MISSION: I will come after you.

SILVER: Put him overboard; no provisions and a pistol with only one shot.

PEW: He's no saint.

MISSION: I won't forget. As God is my witness I won't forget. You'll hang for this, Silver. I'll search out your wife, I'll search out your daughter and if it's the last thing I do with my dying breath I'll serve up their hearts to you on a silver platter.

KEES aims pistol to shoot.

SILVER: No. And take your son with you.

PEW: Oh maybe he is a saint after all.

MISSION picks up HAROLD.

MISSION: God strike you dead, and all Christians turned Turk.

KEES: And remember to tell them who did this to you: Kees de Keyser King of, King of the Barbary Coast.

KEES spits. Exit PEW with MISSION.

What price a saint. I wonder. Take them below.

TOM: Sorry, John.

SILVER: No, no –

TOM: Me and my big foot.

TOM taken off.

SILVER: I'm to be a pirate, I chose to be a pirate.

KEES: And you are a saint.

SILVER: Aye. Yes, I am. He has chosen me to be a pirate saint.

KEES: You can't be both.

SILVER: Sin, the most direct and honest path to God.

KEES: The Devil is our master.

SILVER: Then set me free, bound for England.

KEES: Go back to England and they'll hang you. You'll never set foot there again. You're mine. Take him below.

SILVER: Keep away. I take myself

SILVER taken off.

KEES: Whose side is God on Benn Gunn, the Turk or Christendom.

GUNN: I don't know captain but this I do know if the Turk was so damnable then God would have destroyed him long ago and all his booty with him.

KEES: Damn them, damn them all. Set a course for Rabat Sale Mister Pew, we're going home.

PIRATES: (*Sing.*) **Turn water into wine**
Smite him with fire
Deliver us from evil
Kill the swine

All exit.

FOUR

Enter ANN.

ANN: Mister.

   Silence.

   Mister.

   Silence. Enter MARY.

   He's gone.

MARY: Yes.

ANN: Gone to Hell.

MARY: No. Taken by the soldiers.

ANN: Spirited away.

MARY: Press ganged to over the Great Pond, away, down river, out to sea, beyond Grave's End, without comfort, crying and mourning for redemption from his slavery.

ANN: I sent him to Hell.

MARY: No, he sent himself. Now hurry. This place is not safe for us.

ANN: Where are we going.

MARY: Where we always go when he abandons us – home, Bristol – the town of our fathers.

ANN: How will he know to find us.

MARY: He'll know.

ANN: He's got my ring.

MARY: Stupid man.

   Exit ANN and MARY.

ACT TWO

ONE

Pirate ship. Deck.

Enter SILVER, TOM, each with a broom, PIRATE GUARD. Stop centre stage.

Song: TRIBELESS LANDLESS

PIRATES: **Tribeless, landless**
Nameless and Godless
We wander the earth
Our bellies full and aimless

(*Chorus.*) **We wander the earth**
We wander the earth
Don't know where we're going
We wander the earth

Fearless, wreckless
Shameless and feckless
We wander the earth
Our bellies full and aimless

(*Chorus.*)

BLACK DOG: Grab your brooms slaves. We've reached Africa.

SILVER: So?

BLACK DOG: The slave auction.

SILVER: Oh. The play!

TOM: What play? I don't know anything about a play.

SILVER: That's because you've been passed out these last three months.

BLACK DOG: Three months at sea and I've seen you weep and howl with pain and now, at last, we'll be shot of you.

TOM: What play are we doing?

BLACK DOG: A play about lust, greed, murder, revenge and the killing of kings. And this will be our stage. Now sweep.

SILVER and TOM sweep. BLACK DOG sits and watches.

TOM: Water. Food.

TOM collapses.

BLACK DOG: Leave him.

TOM: Feed me.

BLACK DOG: Do a miracle. No. Whether you be saint or fiend I don't know – but since you came aboard there's been a strange atmosphere and several freaks of nature.

BLACK DOG spits.

Let him die.

BLACK DOG sleeps.

SILVER: Stand Tom, stand. Three months we've been down below, three months at sea to get to Africa for a slave auction that will take the form of a play. Stand Tom, stand. We must stick together Tom, and avoid being separated at all costs.

TOM: Bread. Give me bread.

Enter DERBY with HAMLET in irons.

DERBY: Pew said to let the savage out of solitary confinement. Let him stretch his legs before the play.

HAMLET unshackled. HAMLET howls.

Hamlet, mad dog.

SILVER: He doesn't scare me. You don't scare me.

DERBY: Sweep the stage.

HAMLET: Yes boss.

Fetches broom and sweeps.

BLACK DOG: If he's not standing when I return then it's over the side and feed the fishes.

Exit PIRATES.

TOM: Water.

SILVER: Stand Tom, stand.

HAMLET: Where do you come from.

SILVER: Nowhere.

TOM: What are you looking at.

HAMLET: Nothing. Nowhere. And you made it all the way to here.

TOM: What do you want.

HAMLET: Devil or saint.

SILVER: Believe what you want.

HAMLET: I am a prophet. Your friend will die.

SILVER: Don't listen to him, Tom.

TOM: It's cold.

HAMLET: (*To SILVER.*) You're coming with me.

SILVER: Oh aye, and where are we going.

HAMLET: Where nobody works. A mother in the kitchen and a bitch in my bed.

SILVER: A whore in my bed.

HAMLET: A mother in the kitchen and a whore in my bed.

SILVER: A whore in the kitchen and my mother in bed.

Both laugh.

HAMLET: They call me Hamlet, because of the part I'm playing.

SILVER: I'm to play Horatio.

HAMLET: I know. You will be my friend. (*Whispers.*) When the murdered king gives me the sword that will be the signal.

SILVER: For what.

HAMLET: (*Whispers.*) To escape. My sword will be the signal.

SILVER: And where will our swords to be?

HAMLET: You must turn your ploughshares into weapons.

SILVER: My bare hands.

HAMLET: Better to fight and die like a man than live and work like a mule.

SILVER: Oh, no, no thanks, count me out.

TOM: Yes, count us out – we've got our own plan.

SILVER: Aye, our own plan. What's our plan.

TOM: I can't. It's secret. You'll see.

Enter PEW. They pick up their brooms and sweep.

Song: TRASH AN' WINDMILL

HAMLET: **Trash an' windmill**
　　　　Crack bubble an' beat
　　　　De vat in de fac'try
　　　　Sugar an' wheat
　　　　Load pun me head
　　　　Load in de cart
　　　　Boss got de stick
　　　　An' momma got me heart
　　　　De sins of me father
　　　　An' flood o' de ages
　　　　De lash an' de whip
　　　　Dese are me wages
　　　　Load pun me head
　　　　Load in de cart
　　　　Boss got de belt
　　　　An' momma got me heart

PEW spits on deck.

PEW: Hamlet you black bastard, stop that noise and wipe up this spit.

HAMLET: Yes boss.

PEW: I don't approve of slaving, what about you.

SILVER: You've only got one eye.

PEW: I don't like you.

SILVER: I don't like you.

PEW: You, can you read.

Silence.

SILVER: Yes, he can read.

PEW: Aye, but can he speak.

TOM: I know my ABC.

PEW: Good lad, you can play the ghost.

TOM: Why me.

PEW: You can read and we've lost an actor.

SILVER: What happened to him.

PEW: He got purchased for fifteen guineas during our last showing off the Gold Coast. We should have held on for more, only his acting was so bad we had nothing to barter with. The captain had to let him go to a sugar plantation, when he could easily have gone to an Arab prince or some-such-like for a better price. And all because he didn't act better. So let's have better acting, it's in all our interests. This is your call slaves, set the stage –

Enter PIRATES and SLAVES and set the stage.

It's market day; you're the entertainment and you're on sale.

Enter KEES and GUNN.

GUNN: And two times I came close to him on deck. And both times there happened a shower of rain.

KEES: A valuable commodity in a hot country.

GUNN: Aye, captain. And then there's the bolt of lightning that came out of nowhere from a clear blue sky, pierced the lookout's scalp and burned holes in his feet.

KEES: Bad luck.

GUNN: And then there's the phantom man-o'-war that sailed by in the clouds one morning just after breakfast. About five fathoms up and ninety tons.

KEES: A mirage.

GUNN: And then there's the yam Pew sliced open and found 'God' written all the way through it.

KEES: Damn this saint.

GUNN: The men are so distracted between these miracles and common sense that they don't know what to believe.

KEES: Whatever the outcome of today whether he be sold or not I'll be rid of him.

GUNN: Why captain what are you going to do.

KEES: If he ain't sold I'll cut his throat.

PIRATES: Starboard-side – starboard-side captain – starboard – with the wind in her sails – coming into port –

KEES: You saint, up aft nearer your God and tell me what you see.

SILVER goes up aft. PEW blows whistle.

PEW: The stage is set.

Exit all but KEES, GUNN and SILVER.

KEES: What do you see.

SILVER: A vessel like no other.

KEES: Tell me.

SILVER: Sails of sendal, ropes and tacklings all of finest silk, stems cut of gleaming ivory, planks and sides of cypress wood, the pride of Barbary. A crew of Saracen foes ranting and raving, treacherous, oath-breaking, double-dealing, slaving black-a-moors.

KEES: The Sultan's barge.

SILVER: And beyond that, land.

KEES: Morocco.

SILVER: The gold domes of a city-port shimmering in the heat.

KEES: Rabat Sale. Gunn. When our guests arrive keep a watch for the English French and Dutch ambassadors trying to cut deals behind each other's backs to stop us from attacking their ships.

GUNN: We strike no deals.

KEES: We recognise no authority but our own, any pirate that does different is low-life-back-stabbing-scum and I'll skin alive.

GUNN: I'll keep a watch.

KEES: And remember, if he isn't sold we cut his throat.

GUNN: Aye, captain.

Exit GUNN.

KEES: Saint, what part are you playing.

SILVER: Hamlet's friend, Horatio.

KEES: You have acted before.

SILVER: I once played Julius Caesar in gaol and was slain by Brutus.

KEES: Aye, well cast. Come here, saint.

SILVER: Just John will do sir, captain, sir, just plain John.

KEES: Aye, John. Keep the play simple, John. Our purpose is to entertain while displaying our wares. So we must be able to hear and see clearly our actors at all times. And remember everything is an illusion, nothing is real, words alone will do the violence – we leave the real killings for offstage.

SILVER: And what happens if I'm not sold, captain.

KEES: Don't worry 'saint', I've thought of everything.

SILVER: Thank you captain, I thought you might. Now I'll be able to concentrate more fully on how best to play my part.

Trumpets.

KEES: Here come our slave-trading guests, away and prepare for the play.

SILVER: Captain.

Exit SILVER.

Enter SULTAN OF MOROCCO and beautiful DAUGHTER, slave traders.

KEES: How fares his most excellent majesty the Sultan of Morocco today.

SULTAN: In the market for flesh.

KEES: Good.

SULTAN: What's on sale today.

KEES: Negroes, and a brace of Englishmen.

SULTAN: No Spanish.

KEES: No.

SULTAN: Pity.

KEES: Your father's Holy Jihad has got them too scared to go outdoors, Princess.

SULTAN sits.

We have been gone, gone too long, Excellency. We are returned, returned – a tenth of our booty in return for your protection, Rabat Sale and the safety of her walls. (*Takes SULA's hand.*) All gladly given.

KEES kisses SULTAN'S DAUGHTER's hand.

Princess.

SULTAN: Touch my daughter again, I'll have you killed, you and your pirate republic razed to the ground.

Enter ISABELLE.

KEES: Excuse me Excellency. Isabelle.

ISABELLE: Uncle.

KEES: Niece.

Kisses her hand.

I want you.

ISABELLE: I'm here on business; the English Ambassador has some papers on him that I wish to steal. Details of commonwealth gold shipping routes from the new world.

KEES: I need you.

ISABELLE: Oh look, the Dutch Ambassador is waving. Poor man. He really has got no hair, not on his head, not on his chest, not anywhere.

KEES: I love you.

Enter FRENCH AMBASSADOR.

ISABELLE: The French Ambassador. Hide me.

KEES: Say that you love me.

ISABELLE: The man's preposterous. He thinks that just because I let him lie with me he owns me.

KEES: Monsieur.

FRENCH AMBASSADOR: Monsieur.

ISABELLE: I'll steal the papers and leave them in my purse for you.

KEES: So cold.

ISABELLE: I learnt all that I know from you.

Enter TOM and PEW.

PEW: Captain.

KEES goes to PEW.

The lad has news.

TOM: For my freedom sir and John Silver's. Your word.

KEES: My word.

TOM: I have uncovered a plot among the slaves to mutiny and escape. It is to happen during the play and is to be led by the savage Hamlet.

PEW: I'll cancel the play.

KEES: No we must do nothing to alarm our guests, place armed men round the stage and in the audience. We'll go quell this insurrection with a display of silent strength.

Enter the ENGLISH AMBASSADOR.

ISABELLE: (*Calls to ENGLISH AMBASSADOR.*) The English ambassador. Ambassador.

KEES: Ambassador.

FRENCH AMBASSADOR: You came, sir.

ENGLISH AMBASSADOR: I gave the lady my word.

ISABELLE: Sir.

She sits. They sit either side.

KEES: Let the play commence.

Trumpets.

FRENCH AMBASSADOR: Plays are not against the law for the Frenchman.

ENGLISH AMBASSADOR: A slave market.

Enter SILVER.

SILVER: The King of Denmark is dead. His wife, the Queen, now married to his brother now King and ruler instead. His son, Hamlet, the prince, suspects foul play and doesn't know what to do.

Enter HAMLET.

HAMLET: Good Horatio.

SILVER: My lord, I came to see your father's funeral.

HAMLET: I pray thee, do not mock me, fellow-student;
I think it was to see my mother's wedding.

SILVER: Indeed, my lord, it follow'd hard upon.

HAMLET: Thrift, thrift, Horatio! the funeral baked meats
Did coldly furnish forth the marriage tables.
Horatio! My father! – methinks I see my father.

SILVER: Where, my lord?

HAMLET: In my mind's eye, Horatio.
(*Aside.*) Where's the ghost.
The King my father!
(*Aside.*) Go and get the ghost.

Exit SILVER.

KEES: Make me an offer.

SULTAN: Twenty-five English pounds for your leading man.

KEES: Done. And you madam.

ISABELLE: I like his friend Horatio.

SILVER: Where's the ghost Tom, what's happened to the ghost.

TOM: I can't go on.

SILVER: You've got to.

TOM: I can't.

SILVER: Then I will.

SILVER picks up sword in sheath.

TOM: No, John. I told them about Hamlet's plan to escape in exchange for our freedom.

SILVER: No, Tom. You didn't.

TOM: Aye, I did, a good plan.

SILVER: Turncoat.

TOM: No, I did it for our lives. We're free.

SILVER: Turncoat. We're not sold, they cut our throats.

TOM: What are you going to do.

SILVER: I don't know.

Enter PIRATE.

PIRATE: Get back on stage. I'd like to see you try. That thing's not real.

SILVER: Oh, no.

SILVER unsheathes sword and runs PIRATE through.

SULTAN: Why have they stopped.

ENGLISH AMBASSADOR: Some argument in the plot no doubt.

ISABELLE: He doesn't know what to do.

HAMLET: To be, or not to be: that is the question:
Whether 'tis nobler in the mind to suffer
The slings and arrows of outrageous fortune –
Or to take arms against a sea of troubles,
And by opposing end them? To die: to sleep;
No more; and by a sleep to say we end
The heart-ache and the thousand natural shocks
That flesh is heir to, 'tis a consummation
Devoutly to be wish'd. To die, to sleep;
To sleep: perchance to dream: aye, there's the rub;
For who would bear the whips and scorns of time,
The oppressor's wrong –

SILVER takes PIRATES sword, runs back on stage with swords.

SILVER: Hamlet.

Gives HAMLET a sword.

HAMLET: Saint.

KEES: Pew. Take the other side of the stage. I'll infiltrate the play.

PEW: Aye, captain.

TOM: I'll hide behind this arras.

TOM hides. KEES enters.

KEES: Hamlet, thou hast thy father much offended.

HAMLET: Mother, you have my father much offended.

KEES: Come, come, you answer with an idle tongue.

HAMLET: Go, go, you question with a wicked tongue.

KEES draws sword. All PIRATES follow suit.

Ready, saint.

SILVER: Aye, prince. Now.

HAMLET and KEES fight. SILVER fights oncoming PIRATES. HAMLET and SILVER backed up against the arras.

TOM: (*Behind arras.*) Help, help, help!

HAMLET: Behind the arras, saint.

SILVER: A rat.

Makes pass through the arras.

Dead.

TOM: O, I am slain! John.

SILVER: Tom.

The fighting continues.

ISABELLE: This play's too gory.

She throws herself on the ENGLISH AMBASSADOR.

FRENCH AMBASSADOR: What is Tom.

SILVER rips down arras. PEW pushes TOM forward.

SILVER: Tom.

TOM: Stop the play. Lights, lights, lights.

PEW: You've killed your friend.

SILVER: Tom.

ISABELLE looks up. TOM falls.

ISABELLE: He's dead.

ENGLISH AMBASSADOR: No ma'am, 'tis but a play, never fear.

ISABELLE: Forgive me I forgot.

HAMLET takes the SULTAN'S DAUGHTER and puts his sword to her throat.

HAMLET: Back. Away. Let us go.

KEES: Cut her throat.

SULTAN: My daughter.

HAMLET: She dies.

KEES: Do and you're damned.

HAMLET: Don't and I'm damned.

SULTAN: Give the black devil what he wants.

SULA: Let me live.

HAMLET: Too late.

HAMLET presses sword to girl's throat.

SULTAN: Allah.

HAMLET: Give us our freedom.

ISABELLE: Help me to my bed, hence, ho!

She faints into the ENGLISH AMBASSADOR's arms.

ENGLISH AMBASSADOR: This is what comes of watching plays.

Carries off ISABELLE.

HAMLET: Back. Away.

SILVER: Hamlet. Let the girl go. She's done no harm. She's a child.

HAMLET: The child of the oppressor, the sapling from which grows the rod that beats us and the galley ship that enslaves us.

SILVER: She has not yet chose, he was not of her choosing.

HAMLET: I'll cut her throat.

SILVER: No, cut, mine.

SILVER rips off shirt, kneels.

I offer up my throat instead –

GUNN: A saint.

SILVER: For what blood for what stain for what sin is this child guilty of. What stain, what sin, answer me. Well. There has been enough blood. I surrender, I surrender myself now. I killed my friend, I am worthless, there is nothing left on this earth for me now.

Outstretched arms.

Cut my throat. Better to feast with the Son of God than sup with the Butcher of Judea.

Tilts head back exposing throat.

HAMLET: I surrender.

SULTAN: Praise be to Allah.

KEES: Prepare to meet thy maker, saint.

SILVER: Do it, and do it quick.

KEES levels sword at SILVER's neck.

SULTAN: I, Mohammed the second El-Cheik, Alawi Sultan, Sultan of Morocco, direct descendant of the prophet Mohammed, protector of the Sallee Rovers, believer in God, the one true God, who needs no partners, who has no son, only Him Alone, grant this Christian dog his life and freedom in return for my daughter. See that no harm comes to him and give him whatever he wants.

KEES: My word. Excellency.

Exit SULTAN and DAUGHTER.

GUNN: He's got the luck.

PEW: He's got the luck alright.

KEES: Hang the nigger.

SILVER: He goes with me.

KEES: Straight to Hell. Hang them both.

SILVER: You gave your word.

KEES: I lied. I'm a pirate.

Two nooses flown in.

SILVER: Let fresh eat meat turn in thy bowels and come straight back as vomit –

KEES: Stop that bellyaching.

SILVER and HAMLET gagged, hands tied, black hoods put on their heads and nooses around their necks.

Where's your God now saint. He has abandoned you. Hang them.

GUNN: He's got the luck.

DERBY: He's got enough luck for all of us.

PEW: We hang him and we hang luck.

KEES: I'll hang them myself.

GUNN: I shouldn't do that, not if I were you captain.

GUNN and PIRATES draw pistols/cutlasses.

Give him a choice. If he chooses to go parley with his maker then we'll gladly furnish him with the transport. But if not...

KEES: Saint. Look on the face of God, or sail under the black flag.

Silence.

Hang them.

PEW: No.

KEES: He makes no reply.

PEW: They're gagged.

KEES: Shake your head for life, stay still for death.

SILVER nods yes.

Mademoiselle Isabelle has left her purse.

Picks up purse.

GUNN and TEACH cut down SILVER and ungag him.

SILVER: And Hamlet.

KEES: Do what you like.

DERBY: And this one?

KEES: Let them all go, bad day at market Mr Pew. I'm ashore to give the lady her purse.

Exit KEES and PIRATES.

FRENCH AMBASSADOR: *Sacré bleu!* I am being made a public fool of.

Exit FRENCH AMBASSADOR.

HAMLET: You saved my life.

GUNN: He's got the luck.

PEW: Enough luck for all of us.

GUNN: Look up there lad, what do you see.

SILVER: He has laid his hand upon me.

HAMLET: The sky.

GUNN: Blue.

SILVER: The light of the Lord is our way, and the way of our Lord is mysterious.

GUNN: Now look out there.

SILVER: I am an instrument, I am his instrument.

HAMLET: Nothing.

GUNN: The sea.

HAMLET: Blue.

GUNN: Aye, blue. All manner of different blue.

SILVER: I don't like the sea, I've never liked the sea.

GUNN: (*To TEACH.*) He doesn't like the sea.

TEACH: (*Almost incomprehensible with rage.*) The English have no soul, no poetry, no fire, no passion, puritans and Jew lovers.

Exit TEACH.

SILVER: What's he say.

GUNN: He says that he likes you, he likes you a lot.

Exit GUNN.

SILVER: We have stood before the gates of death, in their shadow, and are saved. He has saved me for some purpose. I have been chosen for some reason.

HAMLET: Lost.

SILVER: Saved.

HAMLET: I am lost.

SILVER: Another country, a forbidden shore where Christians fear to tread. Among outcasts of all nations, all men of desperate and unfortunate condition.

HAMLET: Far away.

SILVER: Hell naked before us.

HAMLET: Far, far from home.

SILVER: Africa.

HAMLET: You are my friend.

SILVER: Tom.

Silence.

The thunder of His power. I am saved for some purpose. Strive not against the will of God, we are saved, the end is truly coming embrace it with open arms.

HAMLET: Your face is sad.

SILVER: I miss my dog. Let's ashore.

TWO

Arabic music. A large prayer rug rolled out across the stage. SNAKE CHARMER, BELLY DANCERS. A proliferation of coloured silks and market traders. The casbah.

BILLY BONES, TEACH, KEES and BLACK DOG sit around a large hookah smoking and playing cards. BILLY BONES is mesmerised by a BELLY

DANCER as she dances for him. Opposite a cluster of Saracens in black with swords.

BONES: His feet.

> *TEACH throws in his cards and goes to rake in the pot.*

KEES: Hold fast, shipmate.

TEACH: I'm not playing.

BONES: His feet, right.

TEACH: I'll only take out the pot what's mine.

KEES: And a feeling I've got says the next card I turn over that pile of booty is mine.

BONES: His feet.

TEACH: You would have that feeling.

> *BELLY DANCER moves away.*

BONES: No, don't go.

BLACK DOG: I don't like the look of those Saracens.

KEES: What are you saying, shipmate.

TEACH: Nothing.

BONES: She's gone.

BLACK DOG: They keep on looking.

KEES: Now pick up your cards and play.

> *TEACH goes to rake in pot. KEES draws pistol.*

One more move and I'll blow out your brains.

BONES: His feet, right –

KEES: What about his bloody feet.

BONES: They'd been neatly severed and placed at the foot of his bed. And no one knows whether this was done before or after they killed him.

KEES: Did he have his boots on.

BLACK DOG: Why don't you just call it evens, eh lads.

KEES: That pot's mine. Was he wearing his boots at the time.

BONES: What time.

BLACK DOG: The time of his death.

BONES: Who's death.

KEES: The man with no feet.

BONES: I don't know, how would I know, what difference does it make.

KEES: A man shouldn't die without his boots on. What have you got on your feet Teach.

TEACH: My boots.

KEES: Good.

Enter ISABELLE.

ISABELLE: There's no need to get up.

KEES: He's calling me a cheat.

ISABELLE: You are a cheat.

BONES: Yes, you are.

Silence.

KEES: Aye, I am.

They all laugh. TEACH joins in. KEES cocks barrel at TEACH.

Who said you could laugh.

TEACH: No one, I'm not laughing, it's not funny.

KEES: No, it's not.

KEES points pistol straight at TEACH, cocks barrel, pulls trigger, swerving it away at last minute and shooting into the casbah among the traders.

TRADER 1: Arrrgh.

PIRATES laugh.

I'm shot.

TRADER 2: You're bleeding.

TRADER 1: I'm dying.

TRADER 3: Call a doctor.

TRADER 1: So much blood.

TRADER 2: He's dead.

KEES, BLACK DOG, BILLY BONES and TEACH laugh.

Enter SILVER, HAMLET and GUNN.

GUNN: So, this is the Casbah then lads.

HAMLET: Ah.

GUNN: And that domed building over there that's the Pirate
    Parliament, where we're headed for; for the Great Debate.

SILVER: A Pirate Parliament.

GUNN: Aye, shipmates, no weapons allowed, we leave all them
    in a pile outside, just the cut and thrust of hearty rhetoric.

ISABELLE: My purse.

KEES: My cabin.

GUNN: Watch your eyes lad, she's the captain's.

SILVER: I miss my dog.

KEES: Where are you going with them.

GUNN: Parliament. For the Annual General Debate.

KEES: What have you got on your feet, lad.

SILVER: My boots, sir.

KEES: Good boy. A man shouldn't die without his boots on.

TEACH: I wonder what those Saracens are up to on the corner.

BLACK DOG: Don't.

TEACH: They keep on looking.

GUNN: The Arab and the pirate get on well in this town. It's
    very good. The average working life of a pirate is three
    years.

SILVER: Then what.

KEES: The gannet's bath.

TEACH: They do, they keep on looking.

BLACK DOG: You start and I'll hit you.

GUNN: We have everything in this town – renegadoes, freebooters, cut-throats, rogues, fugitives of all persuasions.

KEES: And now a saint.

GUNN: Even some of the infamous Indian Thugae.

SILVER: What do they do.

KEES: Kill people like you.

ISABELLE: Ignore him, he's a bad loser.

BONES: You're safe lads – all their killings are calculated; except for innocent bystanders who get caught up in the blood bath.

SILVER: Really.

KEES: Aye, it happened in this square only just.

ISABELLE: I need refreshment, uncle.

KEES: Silver. My mistress, my muse, the most perfect, the most sublime and most precious gem in all Africa, my niece Isabelle.

ISABELLE: Sir.

SILVER: Miss.

Exit KEES.

BONES: Have a puff on this.

SILVER draws on hookah.

TEACH: What do you think those Saracens want.

BLACK DOG: I said don't.

TEACH: I'm not doing anything.

SILVER passes hookah pipe to HAMLET.

ISABELLE: You like.

SILVER: I like.

BONES: Good lad.

SILVER exhales and coughs.

SILVER: I like very much.

GUNN: Now, away to parliament boys, for the great debate.

Exit all but SILVER and ISABELLE.

ISABELLE: You have come a long way. You are a long way from home. To be so far away from those that you love. That love you. A man needs comfort.

SILVER: Aye.

ISABELLE: Sir, you are distracted.

SILVER: The Sultan's daughter, she reminds me of my own.

Islamic prayer music.

ISABELLE: You miss her.

SILVER: Never was there such sweet music in the world before as this.

ISABELLE: Your daughter.

SILVER: Little Ann.

ISABELLE: And without a father.

SILVER: She's safe.

ISABELLE: In a nunnery.

SILVER: With her mother.

ISABELLE: Locked in a nunnery.

SILVER: She's safe.

ISABELLE: There's nowhere safe from the debauchery of men, a constant gaze of lechery and lust. All women a port in their storm.

SILVER: She's just a girl.

ISABELLE: I'm sorry sir if I have given offence –

SILVER: My daughter is safe, no man would dare – the town where she is sheltered I am well known – the town of my fathers.

ISABELLE: It was my uncle that first abused my trust.

SILVER: If any man dare, if any man so much as – there'd be no safe haven for such a man in the whole of south-west

Somerset-upon-Avon – no town, no village, no city – I shall come after him like a whirlwind.

ISABELLE: Calm.

SILVER: Chase him across borders from county to county, rip through England till I have got what I want.

ISABELLE: Calm, sir – she's safe.

SILVER: Revenge, I swear by this ring round my neck which is all I have left to remind me of her.

ISABELLE: Kiss me.

ISABELLE kisses him.

You are my first Englishman.

ISABELLE exits. Enter KEES.

KEES: Hands off Silver. She's mine. That gold belongs to me.

Bell rings.

Parliament.

Exit KEES.

Call to Prayer, led by SULTAN'S DAUGHTER.

SILVER: Such sweet music.

SULA: Are you come to prayer sir?

SILVER: No. I'm a stranger in a strange land. A gentile East of Eden.

WORSHIPPERS: (*Sing.*) **God is most great. God is**
    Most great.
    God is most great. God is
    Most great.
    I testify that there is no god
    Except God.
    I testify that there is no god
    Except God.
    I testify that Mohammed is
    The messenger of God.
    I testify that Mohammed is
    The messenger of God.

Come to prayer! Come to prayer!
Come to success (in this life and the Hereafter)!
Come to success!
God is most great. God is
Most great.
There is no god except God.

SILVER: There was never music in the world like this before.
Never.

THREE

Enter KEES and PIRATES in uproar, throw their weapons into a pile.

Exit WORSHIPPERS. SILVER joins PIRATES.

PIRATES: (*Sing.*) **We don't need rules**
Strong liquor
Aye, no rules
Each man for himself
Gold, belly timber
Punch, rum
Women, booty

GUNN: And a bit of cheese.

Laughter. PEW climbs aloft with two pistols.

BLACK DOG: Rum and a barrel of belly pork for me.

Cheers and applause.

PEW: Order – order – let Calico Jack speak.

KEES: I wouldn't piss down his throat if his stomach was on fire.

Laughter. Pistol shot.

PEW: Let him speak.

DERBY: Put some wind in your sails.

CALICO: We govern ourselves. But in chase and in battle
the captain's the captain. On land he's governed by the
majority. At sea the captain remains the captain for as long
as we permit him to be captain. On land we are captain
over him; he gets no extra food, no private mess or special
accommodations.

KEES: But the captain gets a bigger share of the prize.

PIRATES: Aye.

SILVER: Why's that then.

KEES: Because he's the captain.

SILVER: But if it's equal shares in the risk, if it's equal shares in the adventure, then it should be equal shares in the prize.

Silence.

GUNN: The lad's got a point.

PEW: Aye, the boy speaks sense.

DERBY: Aye, he's clever alright.

SILVER: Equal in all things.

CALICO: Where did you get this idea from, lad.

KEES: England.

KEES spits. All laugh.

We don't need rules, we make the law as we go.

SILVER: You don't like the English.

KEES: I don't like you.

BONES: Abolish work.

PEW: We don't work.

TEACH: Don't work.

BLACK DOG: Whores not war.

GUNN: More cheese.

DERBY: Eat my feet.

KEES: Free whores for all.

SILVER: You all stop paying for it and the captain's mother will starve.

Laughter.

CALICO: You don't pay her do you.

BONES: No, I don't.

GUNN: Me neither.

BLACK DOG: Nor me.

DERBY: Not me.

TEACH: Not I.

GUNN: And not I.

PEW: Not anyone.

SILVER: Only the captain pays his mother for it.

HAMLET: Only the captain charges for it.

Laughter.

PEW: Order, order.

BONES: What about his father.

DERBY: We don't know, no one knows who he is.

Laughter.

PEW: Order.

TEACH: Son of a gun.

GUNN: Son of a fifty-gun salute.

Laughter.

BLACK DOG: He wasn't born he was shot out.

Pistol shot.

Silence.

PEW: The captain's mother is not the question. However, if she is the barmaid at the Bomb and Dagger in Wapping Dock, then she is very likely the mother of most of this parliament, if not all.

Laughter.

SILVER: The mother of all parliaments.

KEES fires a pistol shot. Silence.

KEES: Enough. My mother is the Devil's bitch and she never once dared charge me for it.

All laugh.

PEW: All weapons but mine are banned from this chamber.

KEES: I'm the chief.

SILVER: (*Loud aside.*) A liar and a cheat.

KEES holds up pistol.

KEES: Who said that.

Silence.

TEACH: Him that calls his self a saint.

PEW shoots TEACH.

PEW: First Article of the Fo'c's'le; never betray a shipmate. Take him out.

TEACH's body dragged out.

Your pistol.

KEES: I've got my eye on you.

SILVER: I've got my eye on you.

PEW: I've got my eye on both of you. Pistol.

KEES throws pistol on pile. Cheers from the floor.

Order, order. As you were saying chief, before the mutiny. Your proposal.

CALICO: I amend my proposal in accordance with the boy's idea; equal authority, equal shares and provision for the injured.

KEES: It won't work, it goes against the grain. Each man for himself.

SILVER: Equal shares is each man for himself.

KEES: He can't be trusted. He spared the life of an English Naval Captain, a sworn enemy who vowed vengeance.

Silence.

SILVER: Aye, that's right. And I shot his son. And now he suffers. If alive. And if he is, let Mission come, I'm not afraid. Necessity is my mother. A man must do many things during his life that he will regret, but once done they should be forgot. A man must live his life to the full, and leave dying to the dead.

BONES: Aye.

ALL: Aye.

PEW: All those against.

Silence.

Those for.

ALL: Aye.

BONES: Let's have a bowl of gun-powder punch.

KEES: First, there's a matter I want settled.

Silence.

The 'great powers' offer bribes so as to lay off attacking their ships – I say make no deals.

PIRATES: Aye, make no deals.

SILVER: Take their bribes and still rob them of their gold.

Silence.

KEES: The boy's got bollocks for brains.

SILVER: Why not do both.

KEES: Because they aren't stupid, they'd know who was doing it, they'd see us coming.

SILVER: Attack them under the flags of their enemies and allies, so they don't know who's friend or foe, strike a panic and a terror in the heart of every trader at sea.

ALL: Aye – Aye.

BLACK DOG: He's clever.

CALICO: The boy's smart alright.

DERBY: He's got my vote.

SILVER: And no slaves.

KEES: There's more gold again in slaving.

SILVER: We set their crews free.

KEES: We turn them into profit.

SILVER: It ain't right to treat a man as a donkey or a mule.

KEES: I don't. I charge less for a man.

SILVER: We take no slaves.

KEES: I'll do as I like.

PEW: You'll do as this parliament says.

KEES: To hell with you saint.

SILVER: To hell with you.

KEES: Peasant.

PEW: All those for Kees de Keyser.

Silence.

KEES: You men, we have robbed and plundered the seven seas – choose again. Choose again, I say.

Silence.

Not a man among you. Damn you, damn you all to hell. I sail alone.

Exit KEES.

PEW: What's your name, saint?

SILVER: John Silver, sir.

PEW: And tell me lad, is it short or is it long.

Silence.

BONES: He doesn't know.

DERBY: Show us what you're made of, boy.

GUNN: Aye, give us all a look.

BLACK DOG: Aye, show us what you've got.

BONES: Aye, show us your cock.

All laugh.

Song: SHOW US WHAT YOU'VE GOT

PIRATES: **Are we right, are we wrong**
Is it short or is it long
Don't keep it under key and lock
Come on saint let's see your cock

Can we, can't we
Tie it in a knot

> **Slip knot, reef knot, bow knot**
> **Show us what you've got**

PEW: Well, lad. Don't be shy. Long or short.

HAMLET: Long.

All laugh.

PEW: All those for 'Long' John Silver.

PIRATES: Aye – Silver – aye – aye – John Silver – Silver – Long John Silver!

As PIRATES cheer they fire their pistols in the air, raise SILVER above their shoulders and carry him off singing.

Enter KEES.

KEES: Upstart peasant, bogus saint. Oh, Innocence, I will watch you fall and turn to bitter hate, without compassion, without remorse, alone and full of bile. And if by chance you do not fall – I shall give you a push; a mirror of the man you shall become, a reflection of the boy that I once was. You are my enemy, you are my rival, I will break you.

Exit KEES.

FOUR

Drums. Enter CROMWELL, reading a petition, followed by general HARRISON, OFFICER and GUARDS.

CROMWELL: They call me king. King in everything but name.

Screws up petition.

Parliament. Dissolve it. Let it go the way of its predecessor in the First Electorate, of the 'Barebones' before that, and of the 'Rump' before that. Parliament, my rump. I decide when it sits and when it does not. Tyrant. Traitor to the old cause – one more squawk out of them and I'll put their House up for rent again.

Throws petition away.

Next.

HARRISON: The Humble Petition of the Seamen –

CROMWELL takes it.

CROMWELL: (*Reads.*) '…Disease…bloodshed…wages…
Thraldom and bondage… Impressment… Inconsistent with
the principles of freedom and liberty.' Wages. The wages
of sin. Too much slack. Take up the slack. They get prize
money. What more do they want, these 'able seamen'.

HARRISON: Payment.

CROMWELL: Send them to Ireland, the bastard barbarian Irish
– we should not have stopped, we should have carried on,
we should have wiped them out, till there's not a drop of
living Irish catholic pagan blood left in all of Ireland, driven
them out, into the sea, like snakes.

HARRISON: What shall we say.

CROMWELL: Nothing. Hang them. And Parliament. They say
the Generals grow restless, rumours of insurrection and a
plot to install themselves as the rule of law. What say you
General?

HARRISON: I've heard nothing.

CROMWELL: Nothing?

HARRISON: Nothing.

CROMWELL: Next.

HARRISON: Captain Mission.

CROMWELL: Mission.

HARRISON: Presumed murdered by pirates on The Lion's
Whelp, but lately returned to England after being rescued
off the Isle of Devils, where he was shipwrecked these last
eight years and worshipped by a tribe of savage cannibalistic
pygmies who mistook him for their God.

CROMWELL: (*Shivers.*) A frost.

HARRISON: Send the captain in.

OFFICER: General, sir.

CROMWELL: It's cold.

OFFICER: Call for Mission.

CROMWELL: The glory of God in all it's beauty.

GUARD 1: Call for Mission.

CROMWELL: I'm cold.

GUARD 2: Call for Mission.

CROMWELL: Then Heaven.

GUARD 3: Call for Mission.

CROMWELL: All about me is treachery. Nothing?

HARRISON: Nothing sir.

Enter MISSION.

HARRISON: Captain Mission.

MISSION: General Harrison. My Lord Cromwell, sir.

CROMWELL: You lost your ship, sir, you have been gone eight years and are recently returned from living with pygmies.

MISSION: They mistook me for a God.

CROMWELL: Better they had eaten you.

MISSION: So I have often thought.

CROMWELL: You lost your ship.

MISSION: Eight years since I began this walking death; a corpse consumed, possessed, cold, no life, no blood, revenge my meat, my drink, my sleep, my eat, my staff, my rod, my friend, my reason – curse that wretched night.

HARRISON: A dish too bitter for pygmies to swallow.

MISSION: It was 'Last Dog' watch – we were headed for Jamaica, a cargo of slaves and press ganged labour, when they came at us out of the mist – renegadoes, the devilish Turk Kees de Keyser, my crew mutinied, rose up in armed rebellion led by a cutthroat desperado called John Silver and he shot dead my son Harold.

HARRISON: The pirate saint Long John Silver.

MISSION: He's achieved some notoriety. They pulled me overboard with no provisions and only my dead son for company.

CROMWELL: How did you survive with no provisions?

MISSION: I ate that which was provided, the harvest of my seed.

HARRISON: Many ships out of London have fallen prey to the Saracen's sword, under instruction from this apostate Englishman.

CROMWELL: You had the man and you let him go.

MISSION: He's no man, he's a devil.

CROMWELL: The Devil and the Turk are as one: let it please God to move the heart of parliament and other Christian states, to join together for their speedy suppression and the disjointing of their late strengthened forces, which continually increase by the ships of England and Holland which they daily surprise.

HARRISON: Renegades and Turks.

CROMWELL: Apostates succumbed to sensory temptation and sexual pleasure, paramours embedded in palaces of sin.

HARRISON: Concupiscence, covertness, sodomy, atheism, pampering and fatting themselves with the poison of their unruly desires.

CROMWELL: They plunder our gold, terrorise our shipping.

MISSION: They carry their swords at their sides and run drunk through the towns of North West Africa, not a Christian among them. They sleep with the wives of the moors and when discovered buy their way out of being shot.

HARRISON: They have robbed us of enough gold to pay for the war in Ireland and with the Dutch.

CROMWELL: I want this Silver's head.

MISSION: He's like the wind.

CROMWELL: Human dog.

HARRISON: He enjoys the protection of the Turk.

CROMWELL: The Turk is a scourge sent by God to punish Roman papal pride.

HARRISON: The Pope and the Turk are one and the same thing; the anti-Christ. His spirit the Pope, his flesh the Turk.

CROMWELL: They do think that they are bound to amplify and increase their religion, to compel, to allure, to seduce all mankind, to embrace their superstitions and this they do with all such fire and sword as they can muster in the name of their doctrine and their prophet Mahomet.

MISSION: A danger to the Commonwealth, a danger to Christendom, such a danger that if we do not stamp on this terror and stamp on them hard, we must expect no traffic at sea.

CROMWELL: Then you had better take the Viper, captain – a fifty-gun man-o'-war and stamp on them.

MISSION: Thank you my Lord Cromwell.

CROMWELL: And take General Harrison with you.

MISSION: Sir.

HARRISON: But I'm needed here.

CROMWELL: No. I have plenty of Generals. One less will be good for my health. Get me John Silver.

MISSION: He has a wife and child living in England.

CROMWELL: Then find them.

MISSION: And Kees de Keyser.

CROMWELL: Dead or alive.

MISSION: God be with us.

CROMWELL: They call me King Oliver the First.

Silence.

You have been gone from these shores eight years, what say you that I am.

MISSION: The Lord Protector and saviour of England.

CROMWELL: Well said, sir.

HARRISON: Yes, well said.

CROMWELL: Providence. The providence of God. Everything I do, I do for the Commonwealth of England. The pirate wars against all the world and is the enemy of civilisation. We are at war. A war against piracy.

MISSION: My Lord.

Exit MISSION.

HARRISON: I don't like him.

CROMWELL: He doesn't like you.

Drums. Exit CROMWELL. All exit.

INTERVAL

ACT THREE

ONE

Enter SILVER, with candelabra and candles, cut and bloodied, fresh from a skirmish. Kneels.

SILVER: Lord have mercy upon my soul, I grope in the dark without light and stagger one day to the next like a drunken man I ask nothing for myself, only watch safe over little Ann and grant that I see her before I die. This ring around my neck all I have to remind me of her.

Kisses ring.

Amen.

Enter ISABELLE with candles. SILVER draws cutlass.

Declare yourself.

ISABELLE: Sir.

SILVER: Isabelle.

ISABELLE: In the dark.

SILVER: I pray.

ISABELLE: You are returned ahead of the others.

SILVER: We attacked two bullion ships, The Adventurer and The Charity. But after we had strung up their captains and set about murdering their crews, those ships resembled more a hospital or slaughterhouse, and I could not bear to inflict any more misery. So I let mine go. The Charity. While the others carved up their prey, I let mine go.

ISABELLE: Come to bed.

SILVER: Awhile.

ISABELLE: You pray.

SILVER: Every night – salvation, some sign, every night these last eight years since first I came ashore to Rabat Sale. Eight long years since He laid His hand upon me, since

He chose me as His 'pirate saint', since He chose me as His instrument. And every day I have waited for some sign. Eight years. And every day I wake no clearer as to my purpose, nothing changes, I grow older and I descend further. I am a cutthroat.

ISABELLE: Come, my love.

SILVER: It's cold.

ISABELLE: My lover.

SILVER: I'm cold.

ISABELLE: Here. My scarf.

She puts scarf round him.

You need to sleep.

SILVER: I don't sleep, I can't sleep.

ISABELLE: My love.

Strokes his hair.

Tell me.

SILVER: Nothing. You have arranged a secret rendezvous for me with the English Ambassador.

ISABELLE: Yes.

SILVER: How can we know to trust him.

ISABELLE: You can't. Tell me.

SILVER: He wants to strike a deal so as I lay off attacking English ships.

ISABELLE: Why won't you tell me.

SILVER: There's nothing to tell.

ISABELLE: Then nothing shall be your company.

SILVER: No, don't go. I don't sleep, I can't sleep, I have made many enemies, I am a prisoner.

ISABELLE: Is there nowhere safe beyond this fortress.

SILVER: No port, no safe haven.

ISABELLE: There is one place, a place I know that you have taken to going to each day at sunset – the olive grove by the mosque.

SILVER: Oh, not this again.

ISABELLE: You go there without me.

SILVER: It's a good place, a holy place –

ISABELLE: So I'm not allowed to walk there.

SILVER: Safe from prying eyes.

ISABELLE: Hanging around so that you might catch a glimpse of the Sultan's daughter.

SILVER: She walks back that way from prayer and reminds me of my own.

ISABELLE: Nothing more.

SILVER: No.

ISABELLE: She smiles.

SILVER: No.

ISABELLE: Why not, what's she unhappy about.

SILVER: I don't know…oh, alright – yes, sometimes she smiles.

ISABELLE: And you smile back.

SILVER: No.

ISABELLE: Never.

SILVER: No, never, sometimes – by chance.

ISABELLE: You speak.

SILVER: Never.

ISABELLE: But she looks.

SILVER: Sometimes, yes.

ISABELLE: You look back.

SILVER: No, never.

ISABELLE: Then how do you know that she looks.

SILVER: I don't.

ISABELLE: You find her attractive.

SILVER: No.

ISABELLE: Oh. Maybe you prefer boys.

SILVER: Give me strength, why is it – why is it, tell me…you think like a woman.

ISABELLE: I am a woman. You prefer boys.

SILVER: No, I don't.

ISABELLE: You don't find the Sultan's daughter attractive.

SILVER: Alright, she's pretty.

ISABELLE: So you do, you think she's pretty.

SILVER: Yes, I do.

ISABELLE: Yes, she's pretty.

SILVER: Aye.

ISABELLE: Then from now you pay like all the others.

SILVER: Isabelle.

ISABELLE: No. Sleep with the Sultan's daughter, see what she gives for nothing.

SILVER: She's just a girl.

ISABELLE: Aye, sir, look to that ring around your neck and think of your daughter.

SILVER: Little Ann.

ISABELLE: You've been gone eight years.

SILVER: No, no – no. She's safe.

ISABELLE: There's men your age and older lusting after her youth.

SILVER: No.

ISABELLE: Be mine and mine alone.

SILVER: Isabelle.

ISABELLE: Am I not enough, do I not give enough – I give you all and still you look to others – where are they now – in this room when you need comfort – use your eyes, look harder...I have waited, I have given, and now when it's nearly too late...now you look in another direction.

SILVER: For what. Tell me. For what.

ISABELLE: You would strip me of everything.

SILVER: And what of Kees.

ISABELLE: He's all that I have.

SILVER: You have me.

ISABELLE: I depend on him. When I ask he speaks, when I need he gives, when I want he provides.

SILVER: Aye, you are right – I am chosen for some dark and mysterious purpose, some purpose as yet unknown to me.

ISABELLE: See here, I give – take, take this flesh, my bosom your protection, my heart your salvation – I give you all gladly and in return...no, no I cannot, I will not allow myself to beg.

SILVER: I am a wretch. Betray me for all I'm worth. Only say nothing of my wife and daughter.

ISABELLE: What about me, when do you ever think about me. Kiss me.

He kisses her.

KEES: (*Off.*) Silver.

HAMLET: (*Off.*) Go home old man.

KEES: (*Off.*) I want Silver.

PIRATES: (*Off.*) He sleeps – you're drunk – back – away – keep away –

Insistent banging at door.

KEES: (*Off.*) Silver –

SILVER: Go.

KEES: (*Off.*) Open this door.

HAMLET: (*Off.*) I'll kill you.

SILVER: You want paying, then sell me to the English – they have two strategies to deal with my piracy; bribe me or hang me.

ISABELLE: Never. My love.

Kisses him.

KEES: (*Off.*) Isabelle.

Banging.

SILVER: Go, quickly. He mustn't see you.

ISABELLE: Till later.

SILVER: What place do we meet with the English Ambassador...

ISABELLE: The olive grove at dusk.

SILVER: Trust me.

ISABELLE: Forgive me, I grow jealous so easily.

SILVER: There's no need.

ISABELLE: Lover, love.

Exit ISABELLE.

Doors kicked open. Enter KEES followed by HAMLET, CALICO JACK, BLACK DOG, BILLY BONES, PEW.

KEES: Isabelle.

HAMLET: I told him to keep out.

KEES: Where is she?

HAMLET: I should have killed him.

KEES: Isabelle.

SILVER: She's not here, old man.

KEES: No.

SILVER: No.

KEES: I hear tell that you let your plunder go.

SILVER: Yes, I let the Charity go – I scorned to rob an hospital, to afflict where misery was before, or to make prey of them that had nothing left.

KEES: You lost your nerve.

PEW: And even put some ashore with four shillings a piece to carry them up into the country of Portugal.

KEES: So what does this prove.

PEW: That he's an honest pirate.

KEES: You still cut deals with the enemy.

SILVER: And rob them at the same time. Go home. Put out to sea and pick over the bones of the Charity.

KEES: I don't need your leftovers.

SILVER: Away. Back to your retirement old man.

KEES: I'll do as I like.

SILVER: You'll do as I say.

KEES: To hell with you, saint.

SILVER: To hell with you.

KEES: Peasant.

KEES draws rapier. HAMLET draws his pistol and aims it at KEES.

HAMLET: And I'll blow out your brains.

Silence. PEW, BILLY BONES, CALICO JACK draw swords. KEES picks up scarf off floor on the point of his rapier then sheathes it.

A scarf.

SILVER: Take it, for your wound.

KEES: What wound.

SILVER: Your pride.

KEES: This scarf, it looks very much like one I gave Isabelle.

SILVER: Aye, it's pretty. What. Isabelle's scarf in my chamber. And how would it get here. Come Isabelle has not been here old man. She never was. I was alone at prayer. You are my rival but I'd soon as stab Hamlet in the back than steal your mistress.

Silence.

KEES: Thank you lad. Such kind words. I'm reassured. She's my niece, and I have grown very protective of late.

KEES takes scarf. Exit KEES.

HAMLET: He's like a dog whose fierceness increases with chains, and now set free, let off the leash, will run a course that fiends themselves would shake at.

BLACK DOG: We should have done for him.

CALICO: Aye.

PEW: Aye.

BONES: Aye.

HAMLET: Aye.

SILVER: Never was a man so fortunate as to have so loyal a crew. Come drink with me and then you and me Hamlet, we'll away to do business with the English Ambassador.

TWO

Enter ISABELLE, followed by KEES.

KEES: Isabelle.

ISABELLE: No.

KEES: Forgive me. Please, I beg.

ISABELLE: Not even on your knees.

KEES: Forgive me.

ISABELLE: I gave you all.

KEES: I am a wreck.

ISABELLE: You are a man.

KEES: Wretched, in love.

ISABELLE: You doubt me.

KEES: I adore you.

ISABELLE: You don't trust me.

KEES: I want you to be mine and mine alone.

ISABELLE: Please sir, stand. There is no other man, there are no other men, I tell you all.

KEES: No, not all.

KEES gives her scarf.

ISABELLE: A rag.

KEES: Your scarf.

ISABELLE: Where did you get it.

KEES: I picked it up off the floor of mine enemy's chamber.

ISABELLE: And what were you doing there.

KEES: You deny it's yours.

ISABELLE: No, no, not at all. Why should I.

KEES: So you admit it.

ISABELLE: Yes of course, I love this scarf. It was a present from my lover.

KEES: I gave it you.

ISABELLE: Yes, my love.

KEES: What was your scarf doing in Silver's chamber.

ISABELLE: I don't know. The man's a thief. He can't be trusted. And he smiles too much. What were you doing in his chamber.

KEES: Oh, Isabelle.

ISABELLE: Stupid man. You are my one and only. Banish jealousy, banish doubt. I am yours and you are mine. Another man. What other man.

KEES: I don't know.

ISABELLE: He's in your mind.

KEES: I know.

ISABELLE: The only rival you have is your imagination.

KEES: Isabelle.

ISABELLE: My love.

She kisses him.

KEES: I want Silver dead.

ISABELLE: If only it was possible my love but there's no getting near him, he's constantly surrounded by armed guards.

KEES: I've been watching him. Every day, at sunset he walks alone in the olive grove by the mosque, so that he might see the Sultan's daughter by chance. The fool is besotted with her.

ISABELLE: The man is an imbecile.

KEES: We'll kill him and then sell his corpse to the English.

ISABELLE: No, no he's worth more to us alive.

KEES: I want him dead.

ISABELLE: No, I have a better idea. The lovesick fool. I'll bring the English Ambassador to the Olive Grove this evening and we'll hand him over alive. Let them do our dirty work for us and collect the reward.

KEES: Isabelle my light, my love, my guiding star.

ISABELLE: Oh my dear, my love. You are so much in my heart that all I want is to spoil you, treat you with delights, to see you laugh, and your fine, strong manly face glow with pleasure. Oh forgive me, my love, for being so neglectful.

She kisses him.

Meet me in the Olive Grove at sunset.

KEES: What about the Sultan's daughter.

ISABELLE: Kill her.

KEES: Be it on your conscience and I'll arrange for some scoundrels to stand by so there can be no mistake.

Exit KEES behind pillar.

ISABELLE: My conscience. I will not be held to ransom. Wretched in love, bated by love, a slave to love, you will die for love, my love. I'll cut your throat and sell your corpse as his – better you were dead, for what is life when each day without love is but a little death itself – I am not to blame – I have no choice, all that I do I do for love – I am innocent

– the poison is not the poisoner, the dagger is not the killer, the rope is not the hangman.

Song: MY NEW WORLD

ISABELLE: **My love I am your rock**
    I am your anchor
    You are my compass
    You my silver
    My ocean, my New World
    Your heart is mine

Exit ISABELLE.

Enter KEES.

KEES: Isabelle. Treacherous, cunning, with skills in healing and poisoning, full of malice, fraud, deceit and subtle dealings, without conscience or reprehension.

THREE

Enter FREDRICK and EDWARD.

FREDRICK: This is the place.

EDWARD: You're sure.

FREDRICK: An olive grove.

EDWARD: Under branches such as these that Judas practised his treacherous craft.

FREDRICK: It's not treachery we're up to Edward, it's murder.

EDWARD: Bastards.

Enter KEES.

KEES: Scoundrels.

FREDRICK: Aye, that's us I'm Fredrick. And this is Edward.

EDWARD: Bastards.

FREDRICK: He's Irish. I'm of Welsh origin myself but my voice has been tainted by living in London, though people do say I sing sweetly.

EDWARD: Bastard.

FREDRICK: He can be very convincing in an argument.

KEES: Here comes our target. Hide.

EDWARD: What for.

FREDRICK: It's work.

EDWARD: Bastards.

Enter SILVER and HAMLET. KEES, EDWARD and FREDRICK hide.

SILVER: This is the place, this is the olive grove.

HAMLET: It's not safe.

KEES: (*Aside.*) That's Long John Silver and his best friend Hamlet. My enemies.

He holds up ISABELLE's scarf.

Isabelle. Silver. You're mine. And here comes the Sultan's daughter.

SILVER: See, she walks this way; see, here she comes.

HAMLET: Our appointment.

SILVER: No.

Enter the SULTAN'S DAUGHTER.

SILVER: Good afternoon, young lady.

SULA: Sir.

SILVER: There is no need to fear. We are commercial travellers on our way to a rendezvous.

SULA: What should I fear. I come from prayer.

SILVER: Cutthroats, rogues, thieves, renegadoes and pirates. This country is full of them.

HAMLET: You'd know.

FREDRICK: Let's have them.

KEES: No wait.

HAMLET: Something stirs in those bushes.

SILVER: A bird no doubt. There's one renegado in particular I know, Long John Silver. A fish out of water on land, he wanders aimless communicating in a language that is all heathen Greek to a cobbler; insolent, indolent, debauched, stinking of whale fat and rum.

HAMLET: What would you do if you met him.

SILVER: I'd treat him rough, with cold steel.

HAMLET: I shouldn't like to be in his boots, then.

SILVER: I'd have him on his knees begging for mercy, I'd make him beg and then run him through with my blade.

SULA: He saved my life.

SILVER: You've met the man. Tell me, what is he like. Is he short.

SULA: Oh, no, tall.

SILVER: I have heard he's devilish good-looking.

SULA: Swarthy.

SILVER: Swarthy.

SULA: And rugged.

SILVER: No, don't stop.

SULA: And handsome.

SILVER: (*To HAMLET.*) Tall, swarthy, rugged and handsome.

HAMLET: That was when he was young.

SULA: Oh, no, he still is – I saw him only the other day, here in the olive grove and he hasn't changed.

KEES: (*Aside.*) Here comes Isabelle and the English Ambassador. Oh perfidious Isabelle you deceive me. Isabelle.

Enter ISABELLE and ENGLISH AMBASSADOR.

ENGLISH AMBASSADOR: I see no pirates.

ISABELLE: Over there.

ENGLISH AMBASSADOR: Lovers courting.

ISABELLE: They are your rendezvous.

ENGLISH AMBASSADOR: Well two of them are in love. Pity the poor gooseberry.

HAMLET: Our appointment has arrived.

SILVER: Good day, beautiful miss.

SULA: Good day, sir. I'll sleep safer in my bed knowing there are men such as you go about the country.

He bows, takes her hand and kisses it.

ISABELLE: Which two are in love.

ENGLISH AMBASSADOR: See the way he kisses her hand and she lingers a little too long. Let's talk.

ISABELLE: No wait.

SULTAN'S DAUGHTER goes to exit.

FREDRICK: (*Aside.*) Why does she wait.

KEES: (*Aside.*) Some betrayal no doubt.

EDWARD: (*Aside.*) Bastards.

SILVER: Young miss, before you go. Your name.

SULA: Sula.

Exit SULTAN'S DAUGHTER.

SILVER: Sula. Such sweet music.

ISABELLE: Long John Silver's wife and daughter are in England, they live in 'the town of his father's in south-west Somerset-upon-Avon, Bristol'.

ENGLISH AMBASSADOR: You'll be rewarded for this.

ISABELLE: No more than I deserve.

SILVER: (*Shouts.*) You've come to cut a deal with me sir, so as my master lay off plundering English gold.

ENGLISH AMBASSADOR: I must speak with the pirate Silver himself.

HAMLET: (*Aside.*) I smell a rat.

SILVER: I am an trusted servant of his.

HAMLET: (*Aside.*) Let's away.

ENGLISH AMBASSADOR: I say to a servant go and he goes, come and he comes, do and he does. That is the law of nature. Service is a state of subjection grounded in the curse of sin. Therefore I must talk with your master.

SILVER: Who do you serve.

ENGLISH AMBASSADOR: Cromwell and the Commonwealth.

SILVER: Then your sin must be great.

KEES: (*Aside.*) Now.

Enter EDWARD and FREDRICK. Take SILVER and HAMLET by surprise and knock them out. KEES runs through ENGLISH AMBASSADOR with rapier.

And I relieve you of your service. I cut my deal. We take no bribes.

ENGLISH AMBASSADOR: Call a doctor, wake the apothecary – I am cut, I have been cut. I shall bleed to death.

KEES: No, you won't. Now away and tell your news.

Exit ENGLISH AMBASSADOR.

ISABELLE: After the girl.

KEES: I've got all I came for.

Exit EDWARD and FREDRICK with SILVER and HAMLET.

Silver is mine. Take them away.

ISABELLE: No harm must be done to him.

ISABELLE pulls out knife. KEES puts rapier point to her throat.

KEES: (*To ISABELLE.*) Go on. Do it.

Throws down knife.

ISABELLE: Wretched in love.

KEES: What good ever came of love? No good. Only pain.

ISABELLE: Forgive me.

KEES: Come home with me and we'll have a little parley of our own with a roaring fire and some red hot pokers.

ISABELLE: My love, forgive me, forgive me, save me.

Exit ISABELLE and KEES.

FOUR

Torture chamber. SILVER and HAMLET each bound to a chair. A black hood over SILVER's head. EDWARD and FREDRICK stand guard.

Song: THE BASTARD'S SONG

EDWARD: I am the bastard father
Of a bastard father's son
The bastard son
Of a bastard father's bastard son am I

FREDRICK: He is the bastard father
Of a bastard father's son
The bastard son
Of a bastard father's
Bastard son are you

EDWARD: Am I.

FREDRICK: You are.

EDWARD: All bastards in blood
All bastards in love
All brothers in bastard-hood

ISABELLE screams offstage. FREDRICK and EDWARD stand in shadows.

You wouldn't think she could make so much noise, the size of her.

FREDRICK: In my experience Edward, it's the little women that are most dangerous.

ISABELLE: (*Off.*) Mercy –

ISABELLE screams.

Forgiveness.

Silence.

FREDRICK: They were lovers.

EDWARD: Yes.

FREDRICK: Then this must be a very sad occasion for him.

EDWARD: She cheated him.

FREDRICK: I often find it better to forgive and forget in those circumstances.

Enter KEES with ISABELLE's scarf.

KEES: A rag.

FREDRICK: You're done.

KEES: Heat the irons.

EDWARD: Does she confess.

KEES: I didn't torture her for a confession. A rag. She's done.

Wipes his hands on ISABELLE's scarf.

So much blood.

FREDRICK: Dead.

KEES: Done.

Throws away ISABELLE's scarf.

(*To HAMLET.*) Do women bleed more than men sweet Hamlet, I wonder. Neither man nor beast you are a slave, my slave, you belong to me. Savage. Now I'm going to civilise you. The irons.

EDWARD: Almost a liquid burning fire.

KEES: (*To HAMLET.*) You understand. We understand.

KEES ungags HAMLET.

Confess and I'll go easy.

HAMLET: Do it.

KEES: Where are Silver's wife and daughter.

HAMLET: Never.

KEES: Iron.

HAMLET spits in KEES's face.

What do you want.

HAMLET: Revenge.

KEES: You will suffer.

HAMLET: Gladly.

EDWARD gives poker to KEES.

EDWARD: The iron. Mind how you go, it's hot.

KEES: Over there. Savages, like beasts are the property of their owners, to be indulged or destroyed at will.

(*To SILVER.*) He's holding the iron to his face.

(*To HAMLET.*) Tell me where Silver's wife and child live.

(*To SILVER.*) Save him.

HAMLET: Do it.

KEES: Save your friend. Tell me what I want.

Removes SILVER's hood and gown.

SILVER: I curse you.

KEES: Aye.

SILVER: Just sell me to the English.

KEES: They want your wife and daughter as well; insurance against your escape.

(*To HAMLET.*) Speak.

SILVER: He doesn't know.

KEES: Then you.

SILVER: Take me instead.

KEES: He is your star, he is your friend.

HAMLET: I say nothing.

KEES brands HAMLET's forehead.

KEES: Branded. Save him. Take the iron.

EDWARD: You take it, I'm not taking it, I gave it him.

FREDRICK: Oh, Edward.

FREDRICK takes iron.

SILVER: Mercy.

KEES: No mercy. Hold him down.

EDWARD and FREDRICK hold down HAMLET.

SILVER: For pity's sake.

KEES: Your wife and child. The irons. Tell me.

FREDRICK: Ed, the irons. Now.

EDWARD: Bastard. My back hurts.

EDWARD fetches irons.

HAMLET: Tell them nothing.

SILVER: He doesn't know.

KEES: The irons.

EDWARD: Alright, alright. They're very hot, be careful.

EDWARD gives pokers to KEES.

KEES: Save him.

HAMLET: No.

KEES puts out HAMLET's eyes.

SILVER: How, how, how.

KEES: Undo him.

HAMLET is untied.

You have no stomach for this Silver.

SILVER: Have done with it and give me to the English.

KEES: An end to his groaning.

SILVER: Oh Father, where are you now. Isabelle. You used her wrong.

KEES: She betrayed you, saint. She sold the whereabouts of your wife and daughter to the English. It was her last confession before I cut out her tongue.

SILVER: Kill me.

FREDRICK: Bore through his tongue.

EDWARD: Cut off his hair.

FREDRICK: Slit his tongue, bore it through and brand his head with the letter S, saint.

EDWARD: And cut off his hair.

FREDRICK: Cut off his tongue.

EDWARD: His nose.

FREDRICK: His ears.

EDWARD: And his hair.

KEES: Leave him. Leave him to talk with his God.

Goes to HAMLET.

I examined him before torture, now I examine him between tortures lying down on the rack and with surgical instruments. Bring him to my chamber. Rack him.

SILVER: Savage.

KEES: Look and learn.

Exit KEES. EDWARD and FREDRICK pick up HAMLET.

FREDRICK: He's still alive.

EDWARD: Bastard.

Exit EDWARD and FREDRICK with HAMLET.

SILVER: Father, where are you. I am forgot. In hell. Rammed, damned and lost.

Enter MISSION aloft with flaming torch. Enter ROUNDHEADS below. Flaming torches.

MISSION: We know they are here. (*Reads.*) 'The town of Silver's father in south-west Somerset-upon-Avon, Bristol' – leave no house, no barn, no field, no ditch, no inn, no cellar, no loft, no church, no public gathering, no building, no citizen, leave nothing untouched, leave no one undisturbed, unquestioned, unscathed, wreak havoc, ransack their land, fire their houses, put the fear of God in them, and do not stop until we have found this mother and daughter.

Enter MARY and ANN.

MARY: We are discovered.

ANN: How.

MARY: Put up your hair.

ANN: My father has betrayed us.

MARY: Never. Put on this cap and britches, tie up your hair, bind your chest, flatten it with this book –

ANN: A book.

MARY: Just do as I say – here let me –

She opens the book, lays it flat over ANN's chest and binds it.

Disguise yourself as a boy – go to Ireland, then France and from there Africa.

MISSION: Stop every mother and daughter, every sixteen year old girl and ask 'What is your name', 'Where do you go', 'Who is your father'.

Exit ROUNDHEADS.

ROUNDHEADS: (*As they go.*) What is your name – Where do you go – Who is your mother – Where is your father – What is your name – Where is your husband – What is your husband – Who is your father – What is your father – Where is your father.

ANN with cap on and hair up.

ANN: How do I look.

MARY: Like a boy. Take these britches. Now, go.

ANN: I can't.

MARY: You must. Go now. Go quick. Find your father.

ANN: O mother.

MARY: Ann, my little Ann. Take this letter and show it to no man until you are convinced he is your father.

Gives her letter.

Now go.

ANN: I can't.

MARY: If ever you loved me as your mother, go.

ANN: Mother.

Exit ANN.

MARY: Lord, have mercy upon us.

Enter HARRISON, MISSION and ROUNDHEADS.

MISSION: Seize that woman.

HARRISON: We've got the mother.

MISSION: And the daughter.

MARY: Never. Bind me chattel me strip me naked, withhold
water withhold food, deprive me of light deprive me of
sleep, cut me until I run a river of blood, break my body as
you would a tree. Deprive me of all. And sure as the world
turns, certain as night follows day, the sun rises, the sun sets
– ablaze a constant glory of heavenly light, the fixed point in
our celestial compass – I will say nothing and if I do it will
be a lie. I will take leave of all my senses but I will never,
never let go of that which I love. Never.

HARRISON: She won't say.

MISSION: Then let the interrogation begin.

Exit MISSION and ROUNDHEAD.

Torture chamber. SILVER. FREDRICK and EDWARD in shadows.
Enter KEES with bloody sacking, throws it down.

KEES: Hamlet. Carved well. Meat on the bone, just the skin
removed.

Throws down pouch and a large book.

Ears, nose, tongue and the Holy Bible.

SILVER: When I have done with you –

KEES: Leave him.

SILVER: I will do such things –

FREDRICK: He will come after us.

KEES: Let him.

EDWARD: Bastard.

KEES: You could have saved him, saint.

SILVER: Such things as-yet-unheard-of – then I will bury you
in the cold earth, worms will feed on you sweetly, and you
shall be remembered no more.

KEES: Let it come quickly.

Picks up the Bible.

Hold his hand out flat on this Bible.

SILVER makes it difficult.

FREDRICK: He won't keep still.

EDWARD: I'll choke him a bit.

EDWARD chokes SILVER. FREDRICK presses SILVER's hand flat on the Bible.

FREDRICK: That's it.

EDWARD: He's a monkey and no mistake.

KEES chops off SILVER's little finger.

KEES: I take this finger as severance. Twenty pieces of silver. The ring from round his neck.

FREDRICK rips off the ring, gives it to KEES.

Pretty little thing.

SILVER: No, take everything I have, all that I've got I give, only leave me the ring.

KEES: This is all you've got left to give.

KEES slips gold ring onto severed finger.

With this ring I thee wed, till death do us part. And I'm going to give you the choice. What's it to be, saint. What do you want. Life or death.

SILVER: Revenge.

KEES: Good lad.

Kicks SILVER.

Kick him.

EDWARD and FREDRICK give SILVER a kicking.

Enough. Come and get me, saint, when you can. Meanwhile I'll go about my business robbing and slaving without interference. I set you free, only to watch you fall. Let him go.

Kicks SILVER. Exit KEES. EDWARD and FREDRICK untie SILVER.

EDWARD: Bastard.

They exit. SILVER unwraps sacking.

SILVER: I am plagued, I am rotted, I am perished – the house
I dwelt in was locked to me, my wife forsook me, I lost my
child, I was taken prisoner, I was betrayed, I was made a
slave, lost my country, I was nearly hung, I killed my friend,
I am an exile and a cut-throat. I was saved. I called you
father. And now. To lose all. I called you father. And now.
Did he deserve no better, do we deserve no better. Was I
saved for this. Hamlet. My friend. Better you had hanged.
There would have been more comfort in it. You take too
little care. You took too little care. And now. I am lost. And
now. I fall.

SILVER lifts HAMLET.

We rise and heaven falls. I rise in darkness, without mercy
without pity, I am truly my father's son. As they give birth
we die.

Exit SILVER.

Enter MISSION and HARRISON.

MISSION: A towel, fetch me a towel, to wipe away this bloody
deed.

HARRISON: Well.

MISSION: She chose to break all earth bound ties. Her spirit has
left the flesh.

HARRISON: She said nothing.

SOLDIER brings in towel.

MISSION: The daughter's gone, gone to Rabat Sale, that Muslim
slaughter-house of barbarous cruelty and savage barbarism,
a miserable doleful dungeon for any civilised Christian.
Gone to find her father, God help her, God help us all.

Exit MISSION. Exit HARRISON.

ACT FOUR

ONE

The Cupidos. On deck CALICO JACK, PEW, GUNN, BILLY BONES, DERBY, lying about smoking pipes, drinking rum.

Song: TRIBELESS, LANDLESS

PIRATES: **Tribeless, landless**
Nameless and Godless
We wander the earth
Our bellies full and aimless

(*Chorus.*) **We wander the earth**
We wander the earth
Don't know where we're going
We wander the earth

Brainless, legless
Clueless and hapless
We wander the earth
Our bellies full and aimless

(*Chorus.*)

PEW: Ben Gunn.

GUNN: Aye, One Eyed Pew.

PEW: Nothing.

Silence.

BONES: I'm hungry.

CALICO: Six weeks and still no wind.

PEW: A Jonah on board.

BONES: I'm starved. What's in the galley.

PEW: Potatoes.

CALICO: What's for dinner.

PEW: Potatoes.

Silence.

Ben Gunn.

GUNN: Yes, Mister Pew.

PEW: Nothing.

Silence.

BONES: But what's for pudding.

PEW: Potatoes.

CALICO: Enough's enough. Six weeks since we last set sail, not since poor Hamlet got skinned alive. He's not looking after us. What we need is a new captain.

ALL: Aye – aye – aye – aye – aye.

CALICO: So, who'll it be, then.

Silence.

Not a man among us. Then we'll rot.

PEW: Ben Gunn.

GUNN: Yes, Mister Pew.

PEW: May I have a bit of cheese.

GUNN: One Eyed Pew.

PEW: Yes, Ben Gunn.

GUNN: Fuck off.

Enter BLACK DOG followed by SILVER.

SILVER: You were the watch.

BLACK DOG: Aye.

SILVER: And nothing stirred. Not even a breeze. No footsteps on the bridge. No shouts in the dark.

BLACK DOG: For what?

SILVER: Nothing.

BLACK DOG: Six weeks now, and still no wind.

SILVER: No one's said anything?

BLACK DOG: About what?

SILVER: Nothing. No one's been asking.

BLACK DOG: What for?

SILVER: No reason. You're sure.

BLACK DOG: Why, what have you done.

SILVER: I'm dangerous.

BLACK DOG: You have the fever.

SILVER: My hand, I can't feel my hand.

Holds up hand.

How many fingers do you see.

BLACK DOG: As many as you.

SILVER: Lie to me boy and I'll slit your throat. I'll wait. Wait
for them to come. Who they are I do not know. They never
come, and I wait. One of them in particular I know has only
just recently lost a finger, they took his home, they enclosed
his land, he lost his wife, he had a daughter, they made him
a slave, he murdered his best friend, and watched another
die most horribly – this man reminds me of another man,
some other man –

BLACK DOG: What other man, there is no other man.

SILVER: You see a man like that, you tell me.

BLACK DOG: What's he after.

SILVER: Nothing. He carries 'the blackspot'. Get me a drink.

BLACK DOG: What does he want.

SILVER: To give me the blackspot.

BLACK DOG: The blackspot of death.

SILVER: We acknowledge no countrymen, we have sold our
countries and are sure to be hanged; it signifies nothing what
part of the world a man lives in, so long as he lives well.
Equal authority, equal provisions, equal in all things, we
make the law.

BLACK DOG: Aye, I'll fetch you your drink.

BLACK DOG exits.

HAMLET enters.

HAMLET: John Silver, it's Long John Silver you're after.

SILVER: Aye matey.

HAMLET: The most absolute, the most resolute, the most undauntedest man in fight, that ever any heart did accompany at sea.

SILVER: Aye that's the man.

HAMLET: No, I don't know him.

SILVER: I had him last on the deck of The Lion's Whelp, years back.

HAMLET: What do you want him for.

SILVER: A good look.

HAMLET: Revenge.

SILVER: My hands are tied, bound in dry dock by the heavens – six weeks without wind.

HAMLET: There's a Jonah on board.

SILVER: A Jonah.

HAMLET: Kill him.

SILVER: Aye. What does he look like.

HAMLET: Like a man. Give me your word.

SILVER: I swear.

HAMLET: Give me your hand.

They shake hands.

Don't and it's certain death.

SILVER: I promise. But how will I know.

HAMLET: You'll know.

SILVER: How can I be sure.

HAMLET: Ask him if he is your friend, if he says yes then you know he is lying. Trust no man.

Exit HAMLET.

PEW: The captain's engaged in some deadly argument with himself, ever since poor Hamlet died.

Enter BLACK DOG and FLINT (ANN).

BLACK DOG: Come on boy. Don't be shy. Stand and present yourself. He wants to be a cabin boy. Walked all the way from England.

SILVER: And before that.

FLINT: A butcher boy.

PEW: Another butcher boy Billy Bones.

BONES: A butcher boy you say.

FLINT: Yes, sir.

BONES: Where abouts.

FLINT: Up Pudding Lane.

GUNN: There's a lot of butchers turned salty dog of late mister Pew.

SILVER: Aye, strung up like sausages at Wapping Dock, left dangling on the end of a rope next to God.

BONES: Driven to crime by the foot and mouth, boy.

FLINT: Yes sir.

GUNN: Billy here knows all about butchery, he's a butcher.

BONES: I'm a butcher alright.

GUNN: Murdered his wife, skinned her to the bone and boiled her up with vegetables.

FLINT: Really sir.

PEW: Yes really my laddo, that's why we call him Billy Bones.

SILVER: So, it's a cabin boy you want to be.

FLINT: Sir.

SILVER: What do they call you. Your father's name.

FLINT: I have no father.

SILVER: Nor me, nor me. What became of him.

FLINT: He died.

SILVER: And so did mine. Killed by a man.

FLINT: They call me Roger, Roger Flint.

BLACK DOG: Roger, Roger by God, Roger the cabin boy.

FLINT: Yes sir.

PIRATES laugh.

BLACK DOG: You'll be wanting to come up aft later then, I'll take you up aft and you can bend over and look at the golden nail.

SILVER: Leave the boy alone. You want to be a sailor.

FLINT: Aye, sir.

CALICO: He wants to join us.

GUNN: We're not sailors lad.

PEW: We're pirates.

GUNN: Aye.

SILVER: Tell me boy, are you my friend.

FLINT: I could be sir.

SILVER: But are you. Think, lad – your life may depend on it.

SILVER draws cutlass.

FLINT: I don't know you, sir.

SILVER: You see lad, I'm looking for a friend.

BLACK DOG: Have you got any rum, captain.

SILVER: Aye.

BLACK DOG: Then I'm the friend you're looking for.

SILVER: Yes, you are. Throw the whelp overboard. Let's have some rum, friend.

ALL: Aye.

All exit leaving CALICO JACK and FLINT. BEN GUNN asleep.

CALICO: Just ignore him lad, he's bitter.

FLINT: Why's that, sir.

CALICO: People associate him with death.

FLINT: And you serve under him.

CALICO: I serve no man.

FLINT: He's the captain.

CALICO: Aye. Long John Silver.

FLINT: John Silver. Long John Silver.

CALICO: Aye, he's the captain.

FLINT: How did he get to be captain.

CALICO: We elected him, by common vote; he's bound to do good to us by articles of the fo'c's'le.

FLINT: What if he don't.

CALICO: The chop. And we vote another, but there's not many want it. That's how come he's still captain. Lost his wits, and his best friend Hamlet, trying to protect the whereabouts of his wife and daughter.

FLINT: But he lost his nerve.

CALICO: No, he held that. It was his mistress that betrayed them.

FLINT: His mistress.

CALICO: Aye, but she's dead now.

FLINT: Pity.

FLINT: I should like to serve such a man.

CALICO: The sea is my master.

FLINT: To get to know him.

CALICO: The sea is my country, it levels all men.

FLINT: I should like that very much.

CALICO: The sea will be my grave.

FLINT: To be captain.

CALICO: Watch your back lad and keep a look out for the blackspot.

Enter DERBY McGRAW, PEW, BILLY BONES, following SILVER and BLACK DOG sword-fighting.

SILVER: Jonah.

BLACK DOG: It's not me.

SILVER: To the death.

BLACK DOG: I haven't done anything.

SILVER: Then die.

Lunges at BLACK DOG. They fight.

BLACK DOG: I did nothing.

SILVER: Jonah's never have, self-pitying mongrels. There's no wind.

BLACK DOG: You can't blame me.

SILVER: I don't. I blame your mother.

BONES: Go on, stick him, captain.

BLACK DOG: And what if there's still no wind.

SILVER: We'll be none the worse for trying.

BLACK DOG: Black Devil.

SILVER: No, we are the White Devil, white devils that have God in our mouths and Satan in our heart.

BONES: There's no God in my mouth.

PEW: Only rum.

SILVER: The white devil that commands and teaches others to do that good with our mouth which it hates in our heart: the white devil that binds others with heavy burdens and hard labour; the white devil that robs and kills with a high hand and an impudent face – ugly odious mean-spirited white devils. And I will rip out your guts with my big white teeth.

GUNN: There's only one thing can make a man so demented.

PEW: What's that, Mr Gunn.

GUNN: Love. The captain's in love.

BONES: Is that right, captain, you're in love.

SILVER: Abandon hope all loved ones ever loved by me for I have abandoned you.

GUNN: In love with the Sultan's daughter.

SILVER runs BLACK DOG through.

SILVER: Jonah. Albatross.

BLACK DOG: A curse.

SILVER: Aye. The source of our bad luck. Now we'll get our wind. Anyone else want a taste. How about you, lad.

Silence.

Well, lad.

FLINT: No, thank you sir.

SILVER: Our luck's about to turn. Help me throw him over the side.

FLINT: Yes, sir.

BLACK DOG: Get back.

BLACK DOG drags himself away across the deck on his belly.

BONES: Leave him to die in peace.

BLACK DOG: (*Dragging himself.*) I'm not dying.

BONES: You're dying.

BLACK DOG: (*Dragging.*) My legs won't work that's all.

SILVER: That's what you call unlucky. What are you looking at.

FLINT: Nothing, sir.

GUNN: He's just a boy.

SILVER: How old are you, boy.

FLINT: Seventeen sir.

SILVER: Seventeen. That's a good age. Seventeen.

FLINT: Aye, sir.

SILVER: Tell me what's it like to be seventeen.

FLINT: Much the same as in your day, sir.

SILVER: Remind me.

FLINT: Why sir?

BLACK DOG: I can't feel my legs.

SILVER: Remind me.

FLINT: I am neither a boy nor a man, sir. A man in thought, a boy in feelings. The dreams of a man, the nightmares of a boy. I laugh like a man and I cry like a boy. I drink like a man and I puke like a boy. Lost between boyhood and manhood in the heart of some strange and unfamiliar land.

SILVER: All at sea.

FLINT: Aye, captain.

BLACK DOG: My arms have gone.

SILVER: Do you think it's the same for a girl.

FLINT: Why, captain.

SILVER: No reason.

FLINT: It's the same for girls. Only sooner, sir.

SILVER: You're sure.

FLINT: Aye, sir.

BLACK DOG: I don't feel right lads.

SILVER: What's this…on my hands – bestir, bestir – snares all about me, sudden fears – my blood…liquid fire, burning hell – I have supped the poisoned milk of asps – the blood of others, the venom of their vipers' tongues shall slay me…rise up, rise up – what's the point, there is no point – the arms of the fatherless have been cut off… I am lost. Adrift. Adieu.

Exit SILVER.

GUNN: He's lost his soul.

BLACK DOG: Now I don't feel nothing.

BONES: You're dying.

BLACK DOG: I aren't dead yet.

BILLY BONES sticks him with his cutlass.

BONES: You are now, matey.

BLACK DOG: Bastard.

Dies.

BONES: Give me a hand lad. He could have gone on like that for days.

BILLY BONES and FLINT throw BLACK DOG overboard.

GUNN: It's blue, the sky's all blue.

BONES: As sure as eggs is eggs I'll end up dancing to the four winds.

GUNN: We all have to kick the bucket sometime.

DERBY: Aye.

BONES: Aye.

CALICO: Aye.

GUNN: Aye.

PEW: Aye.

FLINT: Aye.

DERBY: Death waits for no man, Death does not knock, Death comes right in, pulls up a chair and takes what it wants, a ravenous hunger and thirst for life.

Exit DERBY.

BONES: And then what.

GUNN: Paradise mate, paradise – a place of delights, all kind of fruit of all seasons, rivers running with wine, milk and honey, beautiful palaces and fine great mansions, precious stones, gold and silver and every man shall have four score wives, beautiful damsels, and he shall lie with them whenever he wishes, and he shall always find them virgins.

Unwraps a small cloth bundle and offers it to FLINT.

Have a bit of cheese.

Splash of body falling in water.

DERBY: (*Off.*) Man overboard – man overboard –

Enter DERBY.

DERBY: Man overboard – the captain burst in the galley cussing and swearing took hold of a sack of potatoes calling it gold and jumped overboard.

GUNN: What's that, what's that I hear flapping up above Mr Pew…

PEW: The top sail, Mr Gunn.

GUNN: A wind. The drought is ended.

All exit.

TWO

Courtyard of mosque. Islamic music. Muslim WORSHIPPERS prostrate at prayer. SULTAN'S DAUGHTER washes ready for prayer.

Enter HAMLET and SILVER, under the bough of an olive tree, SILVER with small sack of potatoes and rope.

SILVER: Such sweet music.

HAMLET: Aye, she's pretty.

SILVER: This gold is heavy.

HAMLET: She's not for the taking.

SILVER: I don't want her.

HAMLET: No.

SILVER: No.

WORSHIPPERS: (*Sing.*) **God is most great. God is
Most great.
God is most great. God is
Most great.
I testify that there is no god
Except God.
I testify that there is no god
Except God.
I testify that Mohammed is
The messenger of God.
I testify that Mohammed is
The messenger of God**

Come to prayer! Come to prayer
Come to success (in this life and the Hereafter)!
Come to success!
God is most great. God is
Most great.
There is no god except God.

SILVER: Such sweet music.

HAMLET: Revenge.

SILVER: When I looked for good then came evil, when I waited
for the light then darkness came. I cry out and You do not
hear, I stand and You do not see.

HAMLET: Revenge is your purpose.

SILVER: This rope is my saviour.

HAMLET: Go on then, hang yourself.

SULTAN stands before the WORSHIPPERS. During following speech
SILVER slings a noose over the branch of an olive tree and makes
a makeshift gallows.

SULTAN: Blessed is God; the Eternal, Absolute God who did
not father anyone, who has no partner, and nor is He the
son of anyone. Deny His existence and the skies will burst,
the earth split asunder, and the mountains fall down in
utter ruin. All that He asks is that we obey Him, follow
His messengers, and worship Him. God did not create us
without a purpose. Ignore the right of God and He will
punish you eternally. There will be a judgement day, the day
of judgement is coming, and on the day of judgement the
righteous will enter His garden. Accept the religion of Islam
before it is too late. That is what God is commanding you to
do. And do not die except as Muslims.

WORSHIPPERS: Glory be to my Lord, the great.
Glory be to my God, the Almighty.

SULTAN: And say to yourself, 'Truly, I am the first of all
Muslims.' May God guide us all to what He loves.

WORSHIPPERS: Glory be to my Lord, the great
Glory be to my God, the Almighty.

SILVER: Never was there such sweet music in the world.

Exit SULTAN and WORSHIPPERS.

HAMLET: I knew you wouldn't do it.

SILVER: I will, I am.

HAMLET: That branch won't take your weight.

SULA: You are come to prayer, sir.

SILVER: No. I stopped to rest under this tree. My cargo is heavy.

SULA: I know you.

SILVER: I think not

SULA: What is your burden.

SILVER: A heavy cargo, mate.

SULA: What is it.

SILVER: Nothing. I know you.

SULA: The Sultan's daughter.

SILVER: Sula.

SULA: Sula.

SILVER: Such sweet music.

SULA: I know you.

SILVER: I was known for some time as the pirate Long John Silver.

SULA: What is your burden.

SILVER: Gold, my gold.

SULA: And this your gallows.

SILVER: Stand back.

Draws pistol.

SULA: Trust in Allah.

SILVER: I am nothing.

SULA: Trust in him who lives and dies not. He who created the heavens and the earth and all that is between in six days and is firmly established on the throne; Allah most gracious.

SILVER: I am a man.

SULA: The apostles he sent were all men, men such as you, men who ate, drank, walked through the streets – men like you.

SILVER: Saints.

SULA: No, not saints, messengers of Allah.

SILVER: I was a saint.

SULA: Trust in Allah most gracious; He saved my life so that I might save yours. Give me your hand.

Silence.

SILVER: It's against my religion.

SULA: What religion is that.

SILVER: Greed – unconscionable greed.

SULA: You have no conscience.

HAMLET: None, all that come near him die.

SILVER: No. Leave me alone.

HAMLET: I'm going nowhwere. Avenge me.

HAMLET sleeps.

SULA: Come.

SILVER: Kindness.

SULA: We'll talk and then I'll leave you to hang yourself.

SILVER: Allah. A little kindness.

SULA: Give me your hand.

SILVER: I give you my gold.

SULA: I don't want your gold.

SILVER: No. I've got nothing to give. What if a person has nothing to give.

SULA: He has himself.

SILVER: What if he can't.

SULA: Then he should urge others to do good.

SILVER: What if he lacks that also.

SULA: Then he should stop himself from doing evil.

SILVER: What if evil is in his blood.

SULA: Then Hell shall be his reward.

SILVER: Then Hell is where I'm heading.

SULA: Allah sent you to save my life when I was child, and I am sent now in the darkness to save yours. It is the hand of Allah, I am your fate.

He gives her the rope. Whistle offstage.

Trust in Allah.

Whistle offstage.

SILVER: They are come for me. My gaolers.

Enter PEW, DERBY, FLINT.

So you've come to take me to the English.

PEW: Look captain, feel the wind. As soon as Black Dog sighed his last breath, the top sail begun to flap and the main sails filled out and billowed. We're ready to sail.

SILVER: What's this I feel upon my face. A breeze. I am saved. If you had not come, it would be too late and I would be dead.

SULA: I was sent by Allah.

SILVER: Allah.

DERBY: And more, Kees de Keyser –

HAMLET wakes.

SILVER: The scourge of men.

DERBY: Kees has been sighted shipwrecked. He was involved in a disastrous trade for Negroes with a caboodle of them commandeering a vessel and giving chase to him, after revenge. Kees, laden with gold, made headway but then they ran into a storm off the coast of Americk and got shipwrecked, somewhere up the Mouth of the Amazon, or so they reckon.

HAMLET: Revenge.

SILVER: How much gold.

DERBY: The biggest English prize to have ever crossed the sea.

HAMLET: Avenge me.

SILVER: All those for going after Kees.

Silence.

All those for going after his gold.

ALL: Aye.

HAMLET: Revenge.

PIRATES: (*Sing.*) **Gold, gold, give us gold**
We can't be bothered to take revenge

Gold, gold, give us gold
Gold in the hold

Whistle offstage. All exit leaving SILVER, SULTAN'S DAUGHTER,
FLINT and HAMLET.

SILVER: I'll be back, I'm coming back.

SULA: Allah go with you.

SILVER: Yes, Allah.

HAMLET: Vengeance.

SILVER: What are you waiting for, lad.

FLINT: You, sir.

SILVER: Make yourself useful and bring that sack.

FLINT: Aye, aye, captain.

HAMLET: Revenge, and then bury me.

SILVER: Aye.

Exit SILVER followed by HAMLET.

FLINT: You're the Sultan's daughter.

SULA: Yes. Who are you.

FLINT: Roger Flint, the cabin boy. How old are you.

SULA: Twenty. How old are you.

FLINT: Seventeen.

Picks up sack of potatoes.

I'll leave you the rope; you might find a use for it.

Exit FLINT. Exit SULTAN'S DAUGHTER.

THREE

Enter MISSION followed by HARRISON.

MISSION: What now, sir. I contemplate our voyage. Rabat Sale. Are you come to waste my time as a drunkard wastes his money and pleasure by pissing it up against a wall.

HARRISON: Cromwell is dead, our voyage must wait.

MISSION: No.

HARRISON: Cromwell is dead. Confirmed by William Petty, chief cartographer of confiscated lands in Ireland, physician-general, professor of music at Gresham College, and famous for reviving the corpse of Ann Green, hanged for murder and pronounced dead until he discovered the breath of life in her.

MISSION: A witch.

HARRISON: A physician and professor of anatomy.

MISSION: He can revive the dead.

HARRISON: Yes. Cromwell is beyond all help.

Enter MESSENGER.

MESSENGER: Sir.

Gives message to MISSION.

From the English Ambassador in Rabat Sale.

MISSION reads.

MISSION: Prepare me a cure for the sea-sickness. We sail for Rabat Sale in the morning. Silver has gone after Kees de Keyser. We'll lurk in wait and catch him upon his return to Africa.

HARRISON: We must wait.

MISSION: The spirit of terror lives among the rogues, thieves, whoremasters and base persons of the world, they wait for

117

no one – they will pull down the mighty and set up men of low degree in all four corners of the earth – neither republican nor monarchist can sleep safe until this terror has been stamped on, stamped on hard. We sail with the morning tide. I'll have Long John Silver's head yet, lopped off and swinging from the bowsprit.

Exit MISSION.

HARRISON: God help us; God help us all; God help England.

Exit HARRISON and PETTY.

INTERVAL

ACT FIVE

ONE

A shipwreck hull and mast on the shore of the Amazon. Native drums.

Song: FEED THE CROW

ALL: **O each man to his gun**
           Each man to a cutlass
           Each man to his sword or a pistol
           There's work to be done
           Let's open the rum
           And clear the decks for action
           When we can't strike a blow
           And we're near dead and done
           Then fire, fire, the magazine boys
           And up we go to kingdom come
           For better to swim in the sea below
           Than hang in the air and feed the crow

SILVER and HAMLET, cutlasses and pistols drawn.

Enter KEES.

KEES: You came.

SILVER: I promised.

KEES: You've come for your little finger.

SILVER: My ring.

Enter HAMLET.

HAMLET: Revenge.

SILVER: No.

HAMLET: Kill him.

SILVER: No. Allah help me.

KEES: The storm dashed us against those rocks and a mighty
    wave lift up our vessel and wrecked it on the beach. And
    then they came, through the mist, out the water, cannibals
    – who, as soon as they saw us present at them, dived

under water to avoid the execution of our shot; and then appearing, gave us a volley of arrows – but we were fierce and took the beach. This wreck is our stockade, it's mast points up to heaven, the finger of blame

SILVER: You lost the gold. There is no gold. Damn and blast you.

KEES: I know why you're here.

HAMLET: Revenge.

SILVER: My ring.

KEES: Your gold.

SILVER: Aye. And Isabelle.

Silence.

KEES: Alas poor Isabelle. I knew that you would come. I waited.

Enter FLINT, PEW, BILLY BONES and GUNN.

GUNN: Where have all the pretty girls gone. Where's the barb-o-col. Where are the lusty young women.

BONES: Let me at 'em.

PEW: I'm not happy.

GUNN: Neither are we, matey.

PEW: I'm definitely not happy.

FLINT: Why, what ails you, sir.

GUNN: Misery lad, he was born miserable. You always expect the worst.

PEW: And I'm always right.

SILVER: Give me my ring and half your gold and we'll leave you in peace.

HAMLET: No.

KEES: You want my gold.

SILVER: Aye, and my ring.

HAMLET: Blood for blood.

SILVER: Allah, help me.

KEES: Others will come.

HAMLET: Avenge me.

KEES: After.

BONES: After, matey, what's after.

KEES moves away.

SILVER: Flint.

FLINT: Aye, captain.

GUNN: It must have something to do with only having one eye, you see everything half cock.

SILVER: Whatever happens shipmate you stick by me.

Gives pistol to FLINT.

FLINT: What's going to happen, sir.

SILVER: Nothing lad, nothing, drink.

PEW: I've got no luck.

GUNN: You've got no luck, I got landed with you.

HAMLET: Revenge.

SILVER: The ring.

KEES: How far are you prepared to go.

HAMLET: All the way –

SILVER: To hell and back again.

KEES: Then follow me.

All fight. KEES and SILVER with rapiers.

A little blood.

SILVER: A lucky swipe. Give up.

KEES: Never. What have I to fear? Only death.

KEES throws down rapier and climbs rigging of shipwreck pursued by SILVER. In the mêlée below BILLY BONES fighting a PIRATE, charged at from behind by another wielding a cutlass.

FLINT: (*With pistol.*) Behind you, Mister Bones.

BILLY BONES sticks on-rushing PIRATE with sword. FLINT shoots the other.

BONES: Well shot, lad.

KEES pulls a pistol on SILVER.

KEES: Come any closer and I'll blow your head off.

SILVER freezes. In the mêlée below PEW held down by two PIRATES while a third takes a poker to him.

PIRATE 1: Stick him like a pig.

PIRATE 2: Take out his eye.

PEW: No, not my eye.

PIRATE 1: Blind him.

PEW: Anything but my eye.

PIRATE puts out PEW's eye with poker.

Arrrrgh, my eye.

DERBY shoots two with his pistols and slaughters the third with his cutlass.

KEES: I am the Devil's apprentice…

Shoots pistol at SILVER. It fails to go off.

Shiver me timbers, it don't work.

KEES throws pistol at SILVER and turns to carry on climbing. SILVER takes out dagger and throws it at KEES. KEES gets the knife in his back.

Silence. KEES turns.

Blood. My blood. Revenge. At last. Good lad.

(*During the following he climbs to the top of the rigging.*) Get back. We come into this world alone, and that's how we leave it. We eat, we breathe, we live, we die. And in all my years, from that first suck of grief to this last dying breath, I've never known any good to come of goodness. But I'm going to go against a life time's philosophy and do you a favour, saint.

At top of rigging.

Look in my eyes, what do you see.

SILVER: Nothing.

KEES: You, lad. That's what you see. I am your future and there's no escape, no relief – it's all so pitiful and brief – you'll come to no good lad, your course is plotted. You've come too far, there is no escape, only death. I'll keep a seat warm for you down below –

SILVER: The ring.

KEES rips off finger from round his neck, takes off ring.

KEES: Look on it more as a separation than a divorce.

Throws ring up into the air.

I was the Devil's blacksmith
My breath the Devil's bellows
My soul the Devil's furnace
My heart the Devil's anvil
Upon which I beat out good
And turned it into bad

I'll tell him your coming.

KEES throws himself off the rigging.

PIRATES: (*Sings.*) We eat, we live
We breathe, we die

SILVER: Which pirate has got that ring.

Silence.

What-so-ever man finds that ring, I make him my partner, in all things for as long as he wants, and I would gladly give my life for him. I say again, what pirate has that ring.

Silence.

FLINT raises his hand.

What is it lad, what have you seen.

FLINT: Nothing sir.

SILVER: Then don't waste my time.

FLINT: I have the ring.

Holds up ring. PIRATES cheer.

GUNN: Looks like you've struck gold boy.

SILVER: There's gold here somewhere lads, let's find it, load up and away back home to Rabat Sale.

PIRATES cheer.

TWO

The Cupidos. On deck. GUNN, PEW and FLINT. GUNN holds a sack, PEW's eyes bandaged.

PEW: What can you see.

GUNN: The coast of North Africa.

FLINT: The Sultan's daughter came aboard this morning and hasn't left the captain's cabin.

GUNN: We bury Hamlet.

PEW: How's poor Hamlet.

GUNN: A bag of bones

PEW: Not too healthy.

GUNN: No. The captain says we can bury him now.

PEW: You gave the captain back his ring, Flint.

FLINT: Yes, Mr Pew. I argued with him to let me keep it but he wouldn't let me.

GUNN: No, lad. There's only one person he'd give that ring to, and that's his daughter.

FLINT: He said he needed it for some other purpose.

Puts sack down.

PEW: Take off the bandages.

GUNN takes off bandage.

All the way, matey.

GUNN: They are.

PEW: Light a lamp.

GUNN: It's day.

PEW: Black as night.

GUNN: Aye.

PEW: No sun, no stars, no moon. Never again.

GUNN: No.

Silence.

PEW: 'Tis a shame.

GUNN: Aye.

PEW: Great shame. Great pity.

GUNN: Pity.

PEW: I'd grown very attached to it, very fond – it was the only eye that I had. Now I've got none.

Silence.

GUNN: You'll need a stick.

PEW: I don't want a stick.

GUNN: You'll fall over.

PEW: Then I'll fall over until I learn how not to fall over.

GUNN: You'll never see again.

PEW: Aye.

Silence.

And then there's, why?

Silence.

I'll tell you what it means matey, I know what this means, it means I have to change my name.

GUNN: No.

PEW: Aye.

GUNN: No.

PEW: Aye.

FLINT: What's wrong with Pew, sir.

PEW: Nothing. It's 'One Eye' that's bothering me. You can't call me One Eye now, that won't be right, that won't look right, what will that look like, I'll look a fool – I've got no eyes, I can't see, I'm blind.

GUNN: You're blind.

PEW: Blind. From now on I feel my way.

GUNN: Aye.

PEW: Blind.

GUNN: Blind.

PEW: Blind Pew. Out of my way. Get out of the way.

Exit PEW.

Enter BILLY BONES and crew.

BONES: Where's the body.

GUNN: What body, there is no body. Just an old sack of bones.

DERBY: Drape it with the black flag.

GUNN drapes sack with black flag.

Silence.

BONES: Now what.

FLINT: Someone say a few words.

BONES: Ben Gunn.

ALL: Aye – aye – aye – Ben Gunn.

GUNN: Alright. Hamlet. He never was much acquainted with civility, the sea taught him other rhetoric – he never spoke low, the sea talks loud…his hands were rough, his headpiece strong –

BONES: And stupid.

All laugh.

Well he was.

DERBY: Stupid with drink.

GUNN: He told a good story –

BONES: He hardly spoke.

GUNN: He was generous –

BONES: You're making this up.

GUNN: He was reliable.

BONES: He always let you down.

All laugh. Pistol shot.

SILVER: He was a drunk and sturdy sailor, of good use to others, of least use to himself and now of no use to anyone. He was my friend. He is avenged. Praise be to Allah. Feed him to the fishes.

Throws HAMLET overboard. All exit leaving GUNN, SILVER and BILLY BONES – watched by FLINT.

Billy Bones.

BONES: Aye, captain.

SILVER: Tell me again.

BONES: A Muslim man, right –

SILVER: Hold on, hold fast, drop anchor Billy Bones – you want something lad.

FLINT: No, sir.

SILVER: You've lost something, lad.

FLINT: No, captain sir.

SILVER: You're wanting for nothing.

FLINT: No, captain sir.

SILVER: So what are you on deck for.

FLINT: There's no law says a man can't stand where he wants.

SILVER: There's no law says we have to do anything, we're pirates.

FLINT: I'd rather blow myself up than submit to any law sir.

GUNN: Well said lad.

SILVER: But you serve your captain.

FLINT: Aye, captain.

SILVER: Then haul me up a bucket of fresh water to swab down my deck with.

FLINT: Aye, sir.

SILVER: And a fresh shirt from my cabin.

FLINT: Captain.

Exit FLINT.

SILVER: Now, Billy Bones, as you were saying.

BONES: It's like this captain, a Muslim man, right – he can take a Christian wife; but a Christian man, right, he can't take a Muslim bride. If we want one of them we have to turn native.

GUNN: Go Turk.

BONES: You turn Turk mate and she's yours.

SILVER: Sell my liberty.

BONES: No, no – look at what your getting.

GUNN: A wife.

SILVER: I've already got a wife.

BONES: Well have another, have as many as you want, it's the law. I've got six. I love women.

Enter FLINT with bucket of water and shirt.

FLINT: Bucket of water, sir, captain sir. And a fresh shirt.

SILVER takes off shirt. Body covered in scars.

SILVER: Then I'm ready.

Starts to wash down torso.

GUNN: He's ready.

BONES: You're sure.

SILVER: You will bear witness for me Ben Gunn.

GUNN: Aye, captain. We'll fetch her up.

Exit GUNN and BILLY BONES.

FLINT: Bear witness to what, sir.

SILVER gives FLINT cloth.

SILVER: Do my back… Well, lad what are you gawping at. Have you never seen a naked man before.

FLINT: Sir.

Does SILVER's back.

Some mighty scars.

SILVER: My log book. A map of the world. A Spanish dagger, Pygmy arrow, Saracen scimitar, the bite of a South Sea cannibal, English grapeshot, a buccaneer's cutlass, a French rapier, Dutch grappling hook, Indian tomahawk, the lash of the Commonwealth.

FLINT: Don't they hurt, captain.

SILVER: No, lad these are the sort that heal.

FLINT: What sort don't.

SILVER: The sort you don't see. Enough.

Puts on shirt.

So, you are to be my partner. What do you want most.

FLINT: To take a ship, sir.

SILVER: And what will you do with her.

FLINT: Sail her straight to Hell captain, or be damned.

SILVER: No, lad no – set a course for home, and sail back into the bosom of your family.

FLINT: This is my home and you my family.

SILVER: We're not family, we're a pack of rogues. I had a daughter, I had a wife, I had everything a man could wish for. But I was blind. If I had in equal measure the same ability to turn the world back as I do to stand it on its head then I should be a lucky man…the things I would do, and what I would say…a pirate's life may be short, but at least it's a merry one. My family dead. The same boat as you Flint.

FLINT: I think I've found my father, sir.

SILVER: I thought he was dead.

FLINT: He was.

SILVER: Dead and now alive, how come.

FLINT: No, he was lost.

SILVER: Lost where.

FLINT: At sea.

SILVER: They've found his body.

FLINT: I have this letter –

Enter GUNN and SULTAN'S DAUGHTER, garlanded in flowers.

GUNN: Are you ready captain.

SILVER: Tell me after lad. You'll bear witness Gunn.

GUNN: Bear witness to what.

SILVER: Will you bear witness.

GUNN: Aye captain.

SILVER: Then I am ready.

GUNN: Ready for what.

SILVER: Be silent and bear witness man.

GUNN: Aye captain.

SULA: You're sure.

SILVER: As sure as my name is Long John Silver, as sure as is my oath, my word, my loyalty, and my love for you as a man. Now what must I do.

SULA: Nothing. Take my hand.

GUNN: So I'm to bear witness to nothing.

SILVER: Hold your tongue.

GUNN: Will there be cheese.

SILVER: Scurvy swab.

GUNN: I'm very partial to a bit of cheese.

SULA: La ilaha illa Llah.

SILVER: La ilaha illa Llah.

SULA: There is no God except God.

SILVER: There is no God except God.

SULA: Muhammadun rasulu 'Llah

SILVER: Muhammadun rasulu 'Llah

SULA: Muhammad is the messenger of God.

SILVER: Muhammad is the messenger of God.

GUNN: Muhammad is the messenger of God.

SILVER / SULA / GUNN: There is no God worthy of worship except God and Muhammad is his messenger.

SULA: Now you are a Muslim.

SILVER takes ring from round his neck and slips it on her finger.

SILVER: With this ring I thee wed.

Exit FLINT.

GUNN: Pay no attention captain, it's just his age.

SILVER: This time I will take care.

SILVER kisses SULTAN'S DAUGHTER.

VOICE: (*Aloft.*) Ship ahoy – ship ahoy!

Enter PEW with spyglass.

PEW: Starboard side – a fifty-gun man-o'-war.

SILVER: What name does she sail by.

PEW: The Viper.

SILVER: The Viper by thunder, Mission's ship. (*Shouts to crew.*) What Christian soever we meet if he submits not upon the first summons or durst be so hardy as to outdare us, if he be taken he shall be made to turn Turk – if not then he should sink in the sea. Let God be on our side today Ben Gunn.

GUNN: The one God and one God alone, without equal, without son.

Enter FLINT with letter.

FLINT: Captain, sir –

SILVER: Down below my love.

SULA: Trust in Allah.

SILVER: Down below.

He kisses her. FLINT rips up letter. Exit SULTAN'S DAUGHTER.

SILVER: What do you want Flint.

FLINT: Nothing, sir.

THREE

MISSION and HARRISON on deck. The Viper.

Opposite side of stage to SILVER, HARRISON with spyglass.

HARRISON: Twenty-four guns.

MISSION: A pirate ship.

HARRISON: She's flying the French flag.

MISSION: We're in alliance with France against the Spanish.

HARRISON: She's coming for us.

MISSION: Impossible, sir.

Takes spyglass.

What name does she sail under.

SILVER: Raise the black flag.

HARRISON: The Cupidos.

MISSION: The Cupidos, at last at last, Silver's ship.

The Viper and the Cupidos.

SILVER: They're flying the colours.

MISSION: Fly the colours.

GUNN: Lace the netting.

BOSUN: (*Viper.*) Let down the fights.

PIRATE: Make ready with the small-shot.

MISSION: Gunner, give them a broadside.

PIRATE: Broadside.

SAILOR: (*Viper.*) Broadside.

PIRATE: A starboard, there.

SAILOR: (*Viper.*) A port-side, there.

PIRATE: Ready.

SAILOR: (*Viper.*) Ready.

MISSION: Fire.

SILVER: Fire.

Broadside: sails, mast, tackle and rigging fall.

Fire.

MISSION: Fire.

Broadside: more debris falls.

The Viper.

A messenger from the Cupidos.

MISSION draws pistol.

HARRISON: With a white flag. Let him come.

Enter DERBY with white flag.

DERBY: My captain requests a ceasefire, so as women and innocents can disembark.

HARRISON: Tell your captain –

MISSION: Tell your captain, no. You must surrender. You must give up your arms. And you must give us proof. You must allow our men on board your ship for inspection, giving free and easy access to all quarters. You must give up all. You must offer no resistance. You must do all this and you will be spared. Surrender or die. That is our reply.

HARRISON: Yes, that is our reply.

MISSION: Go.

Exit DERBY.

HARRISON: Next time leave the interrogation to me.

MISSION: It wasn't a ceasefire he was sent for.

HARRISON: I am your superior.

MISSION: He was sent to spy on our strength.

HARRISON: Speak out of turn again captain, I'll have you thrashed and scrubbing down the galley.

MISSION: Yes, General, sir.

The Cupidos. Enter DERBY with white flag.

SILVER: Well.

GUNN: Let him catch his breath, he's only short.

SILVER: Well.

DERBY: We don't stand a chance. There's an army on board of at least one hundred men. And of what stock I could see they've enough shot and powder to blow a hole clean out the bottom of the sea, a hole so big as to drain away the ocean.

BONES: And what did they say to a ceasefire.

SILVER: We cut no deal.

BONES: I was only asking.

DERBY: Surrender or die.

PEW: Short legs. Look who's talking.

GUNN: At least I can look, you're blind.

SILVER: 'Sblood, what would you have me say? Where are the days that have been, and the seasons that we have seen where we might sing, swear, drink, drab, and kill men as freely as cake-makers do flies? When the whole sea was our empire, when we robbed at will and the world but our garden where we walked for sport? And now to be held ransom by a petty tyrant. Never. Allah will show the way. Give me that flag. Time to parley with the enemy. I have a plan.

Exit SILVER and PIRATES.

THREE PART ONE

The Viper.

HARRISON and MISSION. BOSUN's whistle. Drums.

HARRISON: They surrender.

MISSION: I'll mind my tongue.

Enter SILVER, GUNN and FLINT with white flag. Drums stop.

SILVER: We surrender.

HARRISON: Which of you is Long John Silver.

SILVER: None. He's dead. Died in mortal combat with that rotten pirate Black Dog.

MISSION: You don't remember me.

SILVER: We've had the pleasure of meeting before.

MISSION: The Lion's Whelp. Captain Mission.

SILVER: I was only mugging. Glad to see you made it home after you was so nearly shot captain.

MISSION: I said I would come after you.

SILVER: A man of your word. I feel safe doing business.

MISSION: It was a pleasure doing business with your wife, Silver.

SILVER: How did you survive, with no provisions.

MISSION: I ate my son.

SILVER: A sweet youth as I remember. We are disarmed, General Harrison.

HARRISON: This much is true. They have given up all their arms. My men have looked and can find none hidden.

MISSION: We must look again.

HARRISON: They have surrendered.

SILVER: We are defenceless.

HARRISON: They are disarmed.

MISSION: We only have their word.

SILVER: We surrender.

MISSION: They are pirates, they are Turk.

SILVER: We have no weapons.

MISSION: That's only what you say.

HARRISON: They have shown us.

MISSION: No, they have only shown us where they are not hiding their sabres and their cutlasses, their gunpowder and their gunshot, their pistols, their muskets and their cannons.

SILVER: Our cannons are empty.

MISSION: And we shall blow you out of the water, obliterate you from the face of the earth.

SILVER: We have surrendered.

MISSION: With what proof, what proof have we; if you say that you have nothing to hide then you are lying, if you show us that you have no weapons then they are hidden some place else. We need proof.

HARRISON: We looked and there was nothing.

SILVER: Nothing. Only pistols and sabres and blunderbuss.

MISSION: I want the truth.

SILVER: That is the truth.

MISSION: That you are liars, that you are cheats, that you are swindlers, that you are pirates, cutthroats, Turks, pagan, infidels, worshippers of the prophet Mohammed, the enemy of our civilisation, and want to rob us of our gold.

SILVER: I give my word.

MISSION: Their word is not worth a mouse's turd.

SILVER: You said surrender or die.

MISSION: And you will die.

SILVER: We surrender.

MISSION: There will be no surrender, there can be no surrender, not until they've been wiped off the face of this earth, not until we have brought this Muslim dog to heel and shown him who's master.

SILVER: Hang me and let the rest go.

MISSION: Back to your ship and prepare to die.

SILVER: And I'll take special care to make sure your death is long and slow and painful.

Exit SILVER, GUNN and FLINT.

MISSION: Order the attack.

HARRISON: I will not.

MISSION: Order it I say.

HARRISON: We'll look again…

MISSION: Stand aside.

HARRISON: We gave our word.

MISSION: Aye, the word is God, and God is with us.

Draws sword.

HARRISON: I'll have you court-martialled.

MISSION runs HARRISON through.

MISSION: All that I do, I do for God.

Exit MISSION.

HARRISON: Oh, to have come so far, and for it to have come to this, ignominious under an Eastern sun. And then again not far enough. We promised all England freedom, equal freedom. Cromwell thy progenitor, the New Model Army his power to power, the nettle once grasped, bitten and stung, corrupted and slave to the will of power for the sake of power's own sake. Dressing self-interest up to look in the public good, passing the mantle onto one of your kin, the son and heir, him your chancellor, you, king in all but name. Where are those men with the strength in power to govern without self-interest, to rule with neither the supremacy of the heart nor the head, where body and mind are as one and speak with the voice of the people – Hah! Death comes. We chopped off a king's head and from that blood I fear all our troubles flowed. Now impaled upon a distant shore. A far far cry from England. Violence breeds violence, hatred hate, revenge revenge, this is life in a cold climate, terror under the shadow of death. Hah! Death takes. The final sup. And after we are gone there is no deathly hush, no prolonged cry of silence, the world clamours on – but, love alone is not enough. Now I must away to pray ready to look on the face of the King of Glory eye to eye and finally ask the reason why.

THREE PART TWO

The Cupidos. SILVER, GUNN, FLINT.

SILVER: Down below lad, watch over my bride.

FLINT: I'll stay on deck and fight.

SILVER: You do as I say or I'll skin you alive.

Exit FLINT.

PEW: There's a storm brewing. A whirlwind coming from the East.

GUNN: And how do you know.

PEW: I can see it.

GUNN: You're blind.

PEW: So, you're ugly.

SILVER: Enough of your squawking –

Broadside of cannon shot.

Hell just opened its gates for feeding.

MISSION and crew swing in and slide down on ropes, swords and pistols drawn. SILVER and PIRATES draw swords.

MISSION / CREW: For England – the Commonwealth – and God.

They fight. SILVER and MISSION swordfight. GUNN against the other two. PEW draws pistol and takes aim.

MISSION: We take no prisoners.

SILVER: White Devil.

MISSION: Damn you.

PEW: I've got him in my sights Mr Gunn.

Enter FLINT who joins the fray. PEW shoots. One of GUNN's adversaries drops.

GUNN: Well shot, Mr pew.

MISSION: Devilish moor. Promiscuous Turk.

SILVER: Agent of Satan.

MISSION: Intolerant and constraining.

SILVER: The Turk constrains no one and tolerates all.

MISSION: Freebooter.

SILVER: There is no distinction between pirate and privateer, outlaw and honourable seaman, renegade and loyal subject, this is the age of plunder.

Lightning and thunder: a sudden storm.

PEW: The whirlwind has come, we are in the eye of the storm.

SILVER: Shipmates! Fast to – the topsail, now – Pew, bring her round, down hard – astern, astern.

MISSION: I'm not finished.

SILVER: We're finished.

SILVER throws down sword.

This storm levels all.

MISSION: Blasphemous bawling coward.

MISSION lunges at SILVER.

Thunder and lightning.

MISSION's sword flies out of his hand and he is flung to one side.

I am struck.

Lightning and thunder.

MISSION falls to knees clutching at his eyes.

And again. My eyes. I am blind.

SILVER: It's over.

MISSION: I'll make you pay for this, Silver.

SILVER: It was not me that blinded you.

MISSION: You'll pay, I'll make you pay.

Thunder.

PEW: All is lost.

GUNN: Damn you Pew, you think the worst.

PEW: This is the worst.

Enter BILLY BONES with axe.

SILVER: Down with the top mast.

PIRATE: Aye, captain.

SILVER: Take that axe and cut the anchor.

BONES: Aye, captain.

Chops at anchor rope.

Enter SULA.

SULA: John Silver.

SILVER: Down below. Get below.

PEW: Aye and pray for us all.

BONES: Bastard anchor.

SULA: Hold me.

SILVER: Below I say.

SULA: I am daughter to the Sultan of Morocco.

SILVER: The sea is no respecter of persons.

SULA: Love.

SILVER: Nor love.

Lightning and thunder.

BONES: (*As he chops.*) Father, mother, wife forgive me.

SILVER: Get below.

SULA: No.

She breaks away and runs across deck.

SILVER: No.

BONES: Mercy.

BILLY BONES swept overboard. Lightning and thunder.

ALL: She falls – she's falling – she falls – watch out on the main
deck below.

SULA: Save me.

SILVER: No.

SULA exits. Exit SILVER after her. Crash of falling mast.

GUNN: The main mast's fallen.

PEW: The captain's fallen.

GUNN: How do you know?

PEW: I see it.

GUNN: You can't, you're blind.

SILVER: Arrrgh – my leg – I'm trapped. It's trapped. My leg is trapped.

FLINT: (*Off.*) Father.

MISSION: In the eye of the storm they shout 'Father'.

Swept overboard.

SILVER: An axe. I see an axe.

GUNN: Pew astern, astern – hold fast –

PIRATES / SAILORS: All is lost – she splits – she splits –

The Lord's Prayer and the Call to Prayer said at the same time, during which the following cries are heard.

Enter FLINT.

SILVER: Bring me that axe.

FLINT passes him the axe.

FLINT: Father, save me father.

SILVER: God only helps those that help themselves. I chop off my leg.

PIRATES / SAILORS: We're going down – we're going down – save me, save us, save thyself.

FLINT: Father.

FLINT swept overboard.

SILVER: Praying never did any good. Goodbye leg.

Lightning, thunder.

SILVER chops at his leg.

Curse the bitch that dropped me – curse the bastard that sowed the seed –

(*With each chop.*) A curse – a curse – a curse – a curse – a
curse –

Stops chopping.

I am saved.

ALL: Drowned

FOUR

A raft.

FLINT, SILVER and MISSION. MISSION slumped upright, eyes bandaged.
SILVER unconscious. FLINT bandaging his leg. MISSION comes round.
FLINT pushes hair up under cap.

MISSION: Where am I.

FLINT: At sea. On a raft.

MISSION: Again. What provisions.

FLINT: Nothing.

MISSION: Blind.

  SILVER groans.

  Who is that.

FLINT: Captain Silver sir.

  MISSION pulls a pistol. SILVER wakes.

SILVER: Alive. My leg. Gone. All gone. God have mercy. Flint.
  You saved my life.

MISSION: And mine. Don't move.

SILVER: Mission. Oh, lad, I always feared you were too good to
  be a pirate.

MISSION: God has provided. I'll start with the boy first.
  Listening to you starve to death Silver, while I eat, will be
  my entertainment and an added sustenance…

  Aims pistol at FLINT.

FLINT: I saved your life.

MISSION: I need the food.

SILVER: See what comes of doing good

MISSION: My mind is fixed. I'm going to eat you, boy.

FLINT: Save me father.

FLINT takes off cap.

SILVER: A girl.

FLINT: Your daughter.

SILVER: No.

MISSION shoots FLINT.

FLINT: Father I am shot.

SILVER picks up a broken oar and runs MISSION through with it.

MISSION: Heaven waits no longer.

SILVER: I'll see you in hell.

SILVER gives the oar a final twist and pulls it out. MISSION dies.

Ann, my little Ann – wait for me.

ANN: Come here father.

SILVER: I'm coming.

Takes MISSION's pistol and drags himself over to ANN.

ANN: Father.

SILVER: Ann. I'm here.

ANN: Come, I'll whisper in your ear.

He bends his ear to her mouth. She spits in his ear.

SILVER: You spit in my ear.

ANN: I die.

Silence.

SILVER: She spat. You spit in my ear. Too late. Too late. Wait, my little Ann wait – I'll take you by the hand, one last stroll, as father and daughter to the first day of school, and on the way we'll dawdle, laugh, I'll tell you not to worry, you'll tell me to be brave…then Heaven's gate, one last kiss –

Kisses her brow.

I'll see you in, wave goodbye…make my way down to the other gate.

Puts pistol to head and pulls trigger. Nothing. He throws pistol away.

I will have revenge, such revenge. And nothing else.

Stands using broken oar as crutch. One legged.

We are exalted but a little while and then brought low – Out of the whirlwind…there was goodness…and you let her perish – I am the hawk I am the eagle I dwell on the rock on the crag of the rock pelted by the storm, look down on my prey without mercy without pity I will slay them all – Out of thy womb blasted this whirlwind. Thou hast withheld water from the thirsty, thou hast withholden bread from the hungry, stripped the naked of their clothing – ye comfort us in vain thou art a false image. This was my daughter… I was lost and am now found… Such revenge. I am God, I am the Devil…all nature combined to make this hell-hole mine…a curse. The world is my hostage and I will hold it to ransom…all men are my slaves – I will have revenge, such revenge… I am the apocalypse, I am the anti-Christ, I am the present day terror and scourge of the world, I am man's revenge on man, I am vengeance.

THE END